101
Kid-Friendly
Plants

Fun Plants and Family Garden Projects

Cindy Krezel

 Ball Publishing | Batavia, Illinois

Ball Publishing
P.O. Box 9
335 N. River St.
Batavia, IL 60510
www.ballpublishing.com

Disclaimer of liabilities: Reference in the publication to a trademark, proprietary product, or company name is intended for explicit description only and does not imply approval or recommendation to the exclusion of others that may be suitable.

While every effort has been made to ensure the accuracy and effectiveness of the information in this book, Ball Publishing makes no guarantee, express or implied, as to the procedures contained herein. Neither the author nor the publisher will be liable for direct, indirect, incidental, or consequential damages in connection with or arising from the furnishing, performance, or use of this book.

ISBN 978-1-883052-54-6

Library of Congress Cataloging-in-Publication Data

Krezel, Cindy.
  101 kid-friendly plants : fun plants and projects for the family / Cindy
Krezel.
     p. cm.
  Includes index.
  ISBN 978-1-883052-54-6 (softcover : alk. paper)
  1. Plants, Ornamental--Juvenile literature. 2. Plants--Juvenile
literature. 3. Children's gardens--Juvenile literature. 4.
Gardening--Experiments--Juvenile literature. 5. Gardening--Study and
teaching--Activity programs--Juvenile literature. I. Title. II. Title: One
hundred one kid-friendly plants.

  SB406.5.K74 2007
  635--dc22

                           2007043442

Printed and bound in Singapore by Imago.
08 09 10 11 12 13 9 8 7 6 5 4 3 2 1

Special Thanks

This book is dedicated to teachers everywhere, who channel so much creativity, patience, and kindness every single day. You're amazing! This is especially dedicated to two great lifelong teachers, in whom I have been blessed: Nita Cohen and Estelle Charles. Thank you so very much!

Contents

Acknowledgments

Nothing I write would ever get written without my kind, patient, and brilliant sister, Kyria (she's pretty cute, too!). This piece also benefited immeasurably from the expertise and kindness of Long Island horticulturist Mary Catherine Gutmann and toxicologist Rose Anne Soloway from the National Capital Poison Center in Washington, D.C. The Poison Center can be reached at 1-800-222-1222. It is always better to be safe than sorry!

Thanks again to my patient editor, Rick Blanchette, who must have wondered if he would ever see this book, and to my friends, who must have wondered if they would ever see me again.

But most of all, a very special thanks to all of the kids who are in this book: Jason (who got over his fear of bugs for this book), Max and Luc, Taylor again, Sandra, Hanna, Giuliana, Scott again, Christian and Colin, Jonathon, Olivia, and Chase. Thank you all so much. You make it fun!

Kids are endlessly curious,
basically kind, completely genuine,
and a lot of fun.

Introduction

I have been lucky enough to be gardening with children for the last fifteen years. It is one of the most rewarding things I have ever done. Kids are endlessly curious, basically kind, completely genuine, and a lot of fun. They enjoy messes, are gleeful about the basics of nature, and absorb anything they are interested in like giant sponges. I never get tired of sharing nature with kids. And I never quit learning from them, either.

At the same time, I have found a growing ring of parents and teachers standing at the back of my classes, wanting to learn for themselves and also wanting to learn how to garden with their children and students. This book has been inspired by the many adults who asked me what plants to use in their gardens and how to garden with their kids. I hope this helps.

The most important thing I have to say is: Be safe! There are some great plants that are not in this book, such as hydrangeas, daffodils, and lantana. All are poisonous. Peace lily, one of my all-time favorites, causes a painful rash if chewed. The plants you will find in these pages are all safe, easy to use, and fun in their own way. However, please remember, as my friend Rose Ann at the National Capital Poison Center will tell you, a child or animal can choke on any plant. And there is no way to be sure of individual allergies or sensitivities. So judge the level of supervision you need when working with your children and act accordingly.

The following plants and garden ideas are ones I have used in my programs with children and had success with. They are by no means the only projects, nor the only way to do them. My best hope is that you will use this book as a jumping off point for your own creativity. Write notes in the margins, comment, and discuss your results with other gardeners and teachers. I look forward to a time when you and your children are all such active, involved gardeners that you will show me your garden innovations and your fabulous, whimsical gardens.

Enjoy!

Seeds are a great way for
kids to learn about gardening.

Chapter 1

It All Starts with a Seed

Seeds are a great way for kids to learn about gardening. They come in multitudes of sizes, shapes, and colors, and some even possess beards, bands, or speckles. Some are tiny, like carrot and coleus seeds; some are huge, like bean, watermelon, and sunflower seeds. Some take only days to germinate, while others can take years. There are even seeds that need to be frozen, burned, or scarred before they will sprout. (Don't worry—I haven't included any of these.) Some are nearly foolproof, while others require unbelievable amounts of time and care. But seeds that germinate easily are a great way to introduce kids to the cycle of plant life in a way that lets the kids feel they did it all themselves.

Starting seeds inside in pots, flats, or trays is a great rainy day project, or plant them straight into the soil outside on a nice day. Planting with a child is an easy way to discuss soil preparation, germination, and plant cycles. Next thing you know, your kids know what they are doing and why—and they have enjoyed the lesson. It's the best kind of learning! Here are a few of my favorite plants to start from seed.

1

Clover
(Trifolium repens)

Clover is a round-leaved plant that grows among the grass. It has delicate, little, white flower clusters that can be pulled apart and sucked on for their sweetness. Clover grows quickly and can spread super fast. They are soft to the touch and easy on the feet. Clover is a perennial and spreads with runners. It is often used in grass seed mixtures. Some people consider it a weed in lawns. If you are among them, be careful where you plant this hardy, spreading plant! However, I feel clover is grossly underappreciated. Clover is the shamrock of Irish history—the variety 'Purpureum' is purple and often even has four leaves! It fixes nitrogen in the soil (which keeps plants green). The flowers are lovely to look at, fun to suck on, and are the basis for a delicious honey. Clover is easy to start from seed and is loved by children. I say, celebrate clover!

Projects

+ Holiday Projects—
  St. Patrick's Day
+ Shady Hideaway
  Gardens

Plant care

Clover seed can be bought at most garden centers. The variety 'Purpureum' may have to be special ordered or purchased online. You can keep clover in containers or plant it where the fixed nitrogen can be of use to the plants around it. It does well in full sun to partial shade. Keep clover moist.

Coleus

(*Coleus* hybrids)

Coleus is an annual that features tall flower spikes and variegated foliage. Its foliage comes in a myriad of shapes and colors, from chartreuse green to almost black, from wide and rubbery to almost ruffled. Its flower spikes are purple or white and plentiful, once the plant has achieved a good size. The stems are square, which kids seem to fancy. Coleus is easy to start from seed and great fun to watch, since the leaves become more colorful as the plant matures.

Plant care

As seed plants for kids, coleus plants are nearly perfect. Give them even moisture and warmth, and you will see tiny sprouts within five to ten days, guaranteed. They are equally at home in sun or shade and keep their bright foliage in both. Start them inside in the winter to keep as a houseplant or a few weeks before last frost to transplant outside into the garden. Once they have a few sets of leaves, keep pinching back the tip growth of the plant to the next set of leaves. Two shoots will grow instead of one, making a fuller, bushier plant.

Projects

+ Cutting Gardens
+ Five-Senses Container Gardens
+ Shady Hideaway Gardens
+ Whimsy Gardens

Cosmos

(Cosmos hybrids)

Children and adults alike love this cheerful garden flower. It is a leggy plant with soft, fernlike foliage down the stems; big colorful flower faces of flat, open petals around a yellow, button center; and seedpods that can be stripped into the hand. Though cosmos is an annual, it will reseed all over the garden, something I have always liked about it. Cosmos flowers come in a wide variety of colors from white to pink, golden to red. There are both short and tall varieties. Plant the short and tall together for a mass of vertical color.

Projects

+ Butterfly Gardens
+ Cutting Gardens
+ Plant a Rainbow

Plant care

The seeds are tiny but effective and germinate within seven to ten days. They can be planted directly into the garden after the last frost or indoors five to six weeks before. They prefer well-drained soil and full sun. The taller varieties may need to be staked.

4

© Dr. Tracy Dougher

Kentucky Bluegrass

(Poa pratensis)

Kentucky bluegrass is what almost everyone thinks of when they think "lawn." It is soft on the feet; deep, rich green; and easy to sow. It also germinates well. This perennial forms a dense, green mat that thickens with age and takes well to cutting. For all of these reasons, it is also fun to plant with kids. Plant a cup to make a Hairy Harry (see pages 132–133), or include your child when seeding the lawn, and then let them take ownership of the watering (and maybe someday the mowing!).

Plant care

Grass seed can be sown onto almost any loose soil or into peat pellets. It does not need to be buried; it only needs to have firm contact with the soil. Then keep the soil moist but not saturated. (How often you water will depend on where you are planting and how well the soil drains.) Grass will germinate in ten to fourteen days. Kentucky bluegrass prefers bright light. Once it has gotten 2 to 3 inches tall, it can begin to be cut or mowed.

Projects

+ Holiday Projects— Fall Events
+ Native Plant Gardens

Marigold

(*Tagetes* spp.)

Marigolds light up the garden. The little pompom or almost daisy-shaped faces stand on sturdy stems covered in finely cut foliage. Originally from Mexico, they have been hybridized for over 400 years and now come in many shades of yellow, cream, and gold and in miniature as well as large, cut-flower varieties.

Projects

+ Cutting Gardens
+ Plant a Rainbow
+ Seashore Gardens
+ Vegetable Gardens

Plant care

Marigold seeds are fun to look at—banded and tufted. They also germinate in three to seven days, so they are ideal for young children, who do not usually have a lot of patience. Plant them into pots or directly into the garden after last frost. Cover them with a light coating of soil, water gently, and then watch them grow. Plant them around vegetables, such as tomatoes, that are bothered by pests as an organic insect and animal repellent.

6

Radish

(Raphanus sativus)

Radishes are one of the easiest vegetables to grow. They have rich green, rubbery foliage on the top, and fat, round roots below. Both are edible, though most people are familiar with the bright red, round roots. They offer nearly instant gratification for children. Seeds germinate in three to five days, and radishes are ready to eat in twenty-five to forty days. Their tall, gangly foliage is fun to watch grow, but what is fun is pulling them out by the top growth to see the bulbous root that has grown beneath. One fun and easy project for radishes is to plant them in clear cups, so that the children can watch the plants' growth above and below the ground.

Projects

+ Science Experiment Gardens— Propagation

+ Vegetable Gardens

Plant care

Simply press seeds down into soil, leaving a pinkie-sized space between each seed for the root to grow, and then cover with a light sprinkling of soil. Water, but do not let them sit in water or they will rot. Though not completely foolproof, they are close.

Sunflower
(Helianthus anuus)

With large, yellow-to-brown faces and encircling yellow or orange petals, sunflowers are one of the most recognizable flowers in the garden. Sunflowers are phototropic, which means their faces turn to follow the sun. Native Americans first cultivated these annuals for their edible seeds. There are now numerous sunflower varieties, including some wonderful dwarfs. Sunflowers bloom in late summer, and humans and animals alike enjoy feasting on their edible seeds.

Projects

+ Cutting Gardens
+ Dried Flower Gardens
+ Edible Gardens
+ Holiday Gardens—
  Fall Events
+ Native Plant Gardens
+ Plant a Rainbow
+ Science Experiment
  Gardens—
  Phototropism

Plant care

The familiar, black and white seeds can be easily sown in to the ground in late spring or can be potted inside by a very sunny window. If you have the room, plant some seeds every two weeks from last frost until July 4 for flowers straight through October.

Sunflowers can be planted into the ground after the last chance of frost or planted into pots any time of year. They need full sun and moist, well-drained soil. Their "turning faces" are a great starting point for a science lesson on photosynthesis and phototropism, or even just on how the same things that make us happy make plants happy—such as sunlight, food, and water. Seeds must be pressed beneath the surface of the soil but can also be planted into clear cups with black construction paper wrapped around, so the roots can be seen once they are established.

Chapter 2

Blooming Bulbs

Bulbs are like little suitcases, containing everything needed to grow into plants once given a chance to settle into the ground. Plant spring-flowering bulbs in the autumn and fall-flowering bulbs in the late summer. (Crocuses are technically corms, but the rule still applies.) You will be rewarded with breathtaking plants a few short months later! Crocuses signal the coming of spring, grape hyacinths make a fine topping for mud pies, and tulips nod contentedly in the late spring sun.

© Michael Rose

Crocus

(Crocus hybrids)

Crocuses were one of the delights of my childhood. The tiny faces surface, sometimes through snow, to herald the coming of spring. The little upturned cups, in shades of purple, white, blue, and yellow, surrounding tiny stamens of yellow-gold, are joyful to see after a long winter. The little tufts of thin, grass-like foliage stay on into the summer, reminding us they are there. Crocuses are a staple in eastern and northern gardens, but have no fear—even southern gardeners can force crocus in pots with a little effort.

Projects

+ Bulb Container
  Gardens
+ Cutting Gardens
+ Rock Gardens
+ Shady Hideaway
  Gardens

Plant care

Push the corms two or three inches into the soil, then cover them well. If you have trouble with rodents, you may want to sprinkle the area with a light dusting of red pepper powder or rodent repellent when you are done planting, as rodents like to eat crocus. Each crocus usually produces two to three stems of flowers. Over time, the crocus corm will throw off cormlets, so you will have a larger cluster with more and more flowers.

Grape Hyacinth

(Muscari spp.)

The flower spikes of *Muscari* are miniature pillars of tiny, drooping, bell-shaped flowers, jutting up out of wide, grass-like foliage. The delicate stems of grape-like, violet-blue or white flowers are perfect for tiny, lightly fragrant bouquets or for adorning mud pies. Nothing is more joyful than a flowering field of grape hyacinth in the spring, and nothing is more suited to small hands than planting the tiny bulbs.

Plant care

Plant grape hyacinth bulbs in the fall. Make it a family event—toss a handful of bulbs into the air, then plant them wherever they fall for a natural grouping. Water in, and then wait until spring. They can also be planted into pots, sunk into the ground, and then brought in for early-season forced flowers. *Muscari* does well in full to light shade. Like crocus, grape hyacinth will have two to three flower stems per bulb, but with time the bulbs will grow bulblets, and the clump will grow.

Projects

+ Bulb Container Gardens
+ Rock Gardens
+ Shady Hideaway Gardens

© Ellen Zachos

Snowdrops

(*Galanthus* spp.)

Though not as well known as crocus, these charming little flowers are well worth meeting. The airy, nodding, three-petaled, white-headed flowers look like tiny fairies from afar, nestled into tufts of soft, lilyturf-like foliage. They often bloom through the snow and are the first true sign of spring.

Projects

+ Bulb Container Gardens

+ Shady Hideaway Gardens

Plant care

Plant snowdrops in the fall, 3 to 4 inches deep. The "throw them up in the air, and then plant them where they fall" method works well for these little gems, and they are easy for small hands to hold and plant. They do well anywhere, from full sun to full shade, though they do best in light shade. They can also be forced in pots. Keep them well watered, both after planting and when flowering. A single bulb will produce a single flower, but they reproduce quickly to make tufted clumps of multiple, nodding heads.

11

Tulip

(Tulipa hybrids)

The tulip is possibly the most popular bulb in the world. Its cup-like flowers of tall petals come in almost every color under the sun and stand on top of sturdy stems. Some tulips are fringed, elongated, or parrot-beaked, but the most popular are the classic full, rounded flowers. Tulips make perfect cut flowers. There are two distinct groups of tulips—the original species, which are usually shorter, and the newer hybrids, which include the cutting tulips we are most familiar with. Tulips have been so desired over history that at one time a single bulb of a rare variety went for $10,000! During World War II some Europeans were forced to eat tulip bulbs to survive. Though I do not recommend eating them, they are a wonderful addition to the garden.

Projects

+ Bulb Container Gardens
+ Cutting Gardens
+ Rock Gardens

Plant care

Plant tulip bulbs in the fall in good, rich, loose soil. In southern states, they will need a cold treatment for up to ten weeks (see bulb forcing on page 122), but in the northern regions they can be planted directly into the ground. Most tulips will give a good showing the first year producing single flowers, and then decline over the next two to three years, if they reappear at all. Depending on your summer climate, tulips will weaken with age and you will need to replace them. Squirrels and rabbits like tulips almost as much as humans do, but they like to eat tulip bulbs, foliage, and flowers. Once you have finished planting, dust the soil with a coating of red pepper to deter them.

Kids especially delight in the endless possibilities of annuals.

Chapter 3

Amusing Annuals

Annuals are plants that grow from seed to full-grown plant, flower, make more seeds, and then die, all in one growing season (usually spring to fall). This makes them perfect for most children's attention spans—something new is happening almost every week. The main attraction with annuals is that they flower almost continuously all season long, in a myriad of wonderful colors, sizes, and shapes. No matter what space you have to garden in, you will be able to find an annual to go there. Try them all—use annuals to fill every available container, nook, and cranny! But keep notes on what you plant and where you put it. If you really hate what you plant, don't worry. They will be gone with the cold, and you can try something different next year. Kids especially delight in the endless possibilities of annuals. A trip to the garden center to buy flowers is a high treat for children. So please, adventure with annuals!

© Ball Publishing

12

Tuberous Begonia

(Begonia **x** *tuberhybrida)*

Tuberous begonias have become a staple of the summer garden. Though technically a tuber, they are most easily purchased already started as an annual. Tuberous begonias have wide, fleshy, succulent leaves that demand to be touched. The slightly hairy foliage sits on longish, thick stems and can be variegated, whorled, or even curly like a snail shell, such as the variety 'Escargot'. The single or double flowers look like miniature, plump roses in a wide array of colors, including white, yellow, red, pink, orange, salmon, and apricot, as well as some lovely variegations. Begonias bloom all summer with a profusion of colorful flowers and are excellent in hanging baskets, raised planters, and garden beds.

Projects

+ Plant a Rainbow
+ Seashore Gardens
+ Whimsy Gardens

Plant care

These are true tubers and need to be started indoors before the growing season for best results. They can be bought in early spring as tubers (February or March is best), or young plants can be purchased near the frost-free date. Already started plants are much easier. Begonias prefer partial shade and like neither full sun nor full shade. They prefer moist, well-drained soil and are heavy feeders, so fertilize regularly. Water directly into the soil and avoid the leaves.

13

Black-Eyed Susan Vine or Clockvine

(Thunbergia alata)

This cheerful vine makes a great outer wall for a kid's hideaway and brightens up any vertical wall. Vibrant yellow or gold over-lapping petals surround black hearts on this climbing vine from tropical Africa. The ivy-like foliage makes a lovely backdrop, but it climbs by vining, so give it something to grab onto. Though annual in most of North America, it overwinters indoors well and will come back better each year. Grow in pots or up trellises or supports for vibrant late-summer color.

Projects

+ Hanging Baskets
+ Seashore Gardens
+ Shady Hideaway Gardens
+ Whimsy Gardens

Plant care

This vine needs support to climb up or does well in hanging baskets. Give it full sun or very light shade and regular waterings. Fertilize often through the summer for best flowering.

Brazilian Verbena

(Verbena bonariensis)

No child's whimsy garden is complete without these tall, nodding, bluish purple flowers. Planted among shorter plants, Brazilian verbena stands sentry and laughs in the breeze. The flower heads tower above the thin, flexible foliage. It is a favorite of many of my young gardener friends, as well as mine. It reseeds profusely, so you will find it unexpectedly in the garden in following years. Enjoy it!

Projects

+ Butterfly Gardens
+ Cutting Gardens
+ Whimsy Gardens

Plant care

Tricky to start from seed, Brazilian verbena is best bought already started just after the last frost. It needs good air circulation. Fertilize it at a low dosage throughout the growing season.

15

Canterbury Bells or Bellflower
(Campanula medium)

Most of the young children I garden with instinctively want to touch Canterbury bells' flowers. The lovely white, pink, lavender, and blue clusters of star-shaped bells wave in the breeze like little people. They stand on tall, blowsy, leaved stems that must be planted close together or staked, but a mass of Canterbury bells creates the look of a classic countryside garden. There are also some very nice dwarf forms available. Children delight in both the look of a mass in the garden and playing with the individual flowers.

Projects

+ Cutting Gardens
+ Plant a Rainbow

Plant care

Canterbury bells prefer full sun but will grow and flower in light shade. They like rich, well-drained, but moist soil. Canterbury bells are a biennial, so plant in late spring or early summer for bloom the second year or buy already started.

16

Cockscomb or Celosia

(Celosia argentea)

Kids love cockscomb! It's a great sensory plant. It comes in a bunch of colors, feels like velvet, and looks like either plumes or wrinkled brains. There are tall and short varieties. It dries well, makes an interesting cut flower, and looks playful in a bed with other plants. Celosia is an annual, so it will flower from June into the fall months. The foliage is not much to look at, but the unique flowers more than compensate. Cut flowers for arrangements or to dry, and enjoy long past the summer season.

Plant care

Cockscomb can be grown from seed but are best purchased as seedlings in flats. They transplant best when young. Celosia can be a little fussy, so plant in full sun and well-drained soil, preferably rich in organics. Cockscomb does not tolerate wet soil!

Projects

+ Cutting Gardens
+ Dried Flower Gardens
+ Five-Senses Container Gardens
+ Native Plant Gardens
+ Plant a Rainbow
+ Seashore Gardens
+ Whimsy Gardens

17

Dahlia

(Dahlia x *hybrida)*

Dahlias are some of the happiest flowers on earth. They come in a myriad of flower shapes, from pompom to daisy-faced snowballs, in every color under the sun. There is a dahlia for every possible taste. The flowers stand on sturdy stems and make excellent cut flowers, as well as bedding, border, and container plants. Best of all, there is something about these fat, happy flowers that beckons kids to them. Dahlias are a sure win in a children's garden!

Plant care

Dahlias are either seed grown or tender perennial tubers. With care, the tubers can be saved from one winter to the next. If you prefer not to do the work, buy dahlias as annuals each year. Be sure to write down the varieties you like, or you will have forgotten by the following spring.

Projects

+ Cutting Gardens
+ Plant a Rainbow

Dahlias need full sun and plenty of water and fertilizer. They must have good drainage because if they sit in water, they will rot. They also prefer cool roots, so for best results mulch well when planting.

Dandelion

(Taraxacum officinale)

Dandelions are underappreciated. Most people are so used to seeing dandelions that they do not really look at them or think about them. But kids love them, and these plants have some great lessons to teach us, too. The seed dispersal system of the dandelion is nothing short of genius. The flowers and young leaves are edible, and the flowers are great for mud pies. Dandelions will be around long after we are gone, because, as any gardener can tell you, they are indestructible. So you might as well learn to love them!

Projects

+ Edible Gardens
+ Science Experiment Gardens—Seed Dispersal
+ Whimsy Gardens

Plant care

Dandelions will grow almost anywhere. They prefer full sun and moist soil. The leaves can be cut for salad, though blanching them quickly improves their texture. In the almost unimaginable chance that you have no dandelions, simply bring home a seed head and blow the seeds into your yard. Soon you will have more than you ever wanted, though not more than your children do!

Forget-Me-Not

(Myosotis sylvatica)

Forget-me-nots are one of the sensory pleasures of childhood. They make a low mat of color in the early spring, but never just where you first planted them. They are a readily self-seeding biennial, which will show up in unexpected places. You can never forget them because they keep coming back! Forget-me-nots are a wonderful butter-fly attractor and make good cut flowers. Their sharp, clear blue color (as well as white and shades of pink) will delight you in the garden.

Plant care

Forget-me-nots prefer partial shade and good, rich, well-drained soil. Sow seed indoors in early spring for summer flowers or in late summer for flowers next year, or buy small plants in early spring. Once established, you will likely see them reappear for years to come.

Projects

+ Butterfly Gardens
+ Cutting Gardens
+ Plant a Rainbow

Fuchsia

(Fuchsia x hybrida)

When I was a little girl, I wanted a dress that looked like a fuchsia flower. I probably couldn't t pull it off now, but I would still be willing to try. Like multicolored crinolines under a ball gown, fuchsias twirl and dip in the breeze. Their colorful, multilayered flowers hang on long, arching stems and are perfect for hanging baskets and containers. They are charming and easy to grow!

Projects

+ Hanging Baskets and Container Gardens

+ Plant a Rainbow

Plant care

Fuchsias can be rooted easily or bought new in the spring. They do best in partial shade, where they get light but not hot sun. They need a great deal of water but cannot stand wet feet. Check each day for dry roots and water accordingly. Do not let them dry out! Use a good fertilizer at half strength each week to promote blooms straight through the summer.

21

Gazania

(*Gazania* hybrids)

I have a little friend who was so proud when she learned to recognize her first flower, that she would repeat this mantra: "Gazillions of gazanias," often followed by ". . . all for me!" The striped, speckled, vibrant flowers of gazanias inspire that kind of joy, even in adults, while the sturdy stems and low-to-the-ground foliage give them substance in the garden. The flowers close at night, like little fairies tucking in to sleep.

Plant care

Gazanias prefer light, sandy soil and full sun. They do well at the seashore and tolerate heat and wind. Remove dead flowers for continuous bloom.

Projects

+ Native Plant Gardens
+ Plant a Rainbow
+ Seashore Gardens
+ Whimsy Gardens

Geranium

(*Pelargonium* hybrids)

If you are not familiar with geraniums, you are in for a treat. These wonderful flowers are available in single, double, and multiflora varieties that range in color from white to red to violet as well as bicolors. Equally striking are the fragrant leaves, which can smell like chocolate, mint, or pineapple, and can add color and texture of their own. Victorians used geraniums as herbs and to make tea. They flower all summer and are easy and vigorous growers. No wonder they are a staple of the summer garden!

Projects

+ Hanging Baskets and Container Gardens
+ Edible Gardens
+ Holiday Projects— Summer Events
+ Plant a Rainbow
+ Seashore Gardens

Plant care

Buy in pots at the last frost. Geraniums are well suited for beds, borders, or containers. Plant them in full sun, and water and feed regularly. Deadhead old flower stalks to stimulate new blooms.

Caution: Some people have an allergic reaction to the sap of this plant.

© Ellen Zachos

23

Globe Amaranth
(Gomphrena globosa)

These cheerful, little pompom flowers stick out on their long, thin stems, like strawberries on sticks. They come in shades of white to bright lavender, and pink to red. They are great for flower arrangements and make excellent dried flowers. They are easy to plant, easy to tend, and nearly indestructible, as well as being silly in appearance. Overall, they are excellent beginner plants for kids!

Plant care

The seeds are tricky, so it's better to buy plants in flats after the last frost and put directly into the soil. Globe amaranth has no real pests and tolerates most soils, drought, wet, and wind. It needs full sun for best flowering.

Projects

+ Cutting Gardens
+ Dried Flower Gardens
+ Native Plant Gardens
+ Plant a Rainbow
+ Seashore Gardens

Hollyhock

(*Alcea rosea*)

Hollyhocks are an old-fashioned garden classic and with good reason. They are joyful! The stately spires are preferred egg-laying grounds for many butterflies. They also make wonderful summertime hedges for small children. The flowers come in almost every color except blue and stand on tall stalks decorated with wide, tri-lobed leaves. The flowers start from the bottom and flower up, over a long bloom time, finally ending with a dramatic showing at the top. Since the plants can reach 6 to 8 feet tall, the display is fantastic!

Projects

+ Butterfly Gardens
+ Plant a Rainbow
+ Seashore Gardens
+ Whimsy Gardens

Plant care

Though technically a biennial, hollyhocks are best treated as an annual and bought as plants after the last frost. Plant hollyhocks into good, rich soil in a wind-protected, full-sun location. Water deeply and feed regularly. The taller varieties may need to be staked.If left alone, hollyhocks will often self-seed.

25

Impatiens or Dizzy Lizzies

(*Impatiens walleriana*) and

New Guinea Impatiens

(*Impatiens hawkeri*)

Impatiens are the most popular annual in America and you can understand why. They come in every color under the sun (except blue and black) and in single, double, and multiflora forms. They are easy to grow and prefer shade. Classic impatiens, or *Impatiens walleriana*, have rich, green leaves and fleshy stems. New Guinea impatiens can have variegated foliage and handle more sun. Children especially love impatiens for their seed pods, which look like tiny, brilliant-green worms, then pop open and spray seeds in the early fall. Impatiens often reseed from these "shooting stars."

Projects

+ Hanging Baskets and Container Gardens
+ Native Plant Gardens
+ Plant a Rainbow
+ Science Experiment Gardens–Seed dispersal

Plant care

Buy in flats around the last frost. Plant impatiens with lots of organic material and plenty of room to grow. They will fill in, and they need good air circulation. Keep well watered! They can wilt in a day without adequate water when planted in the full sun. In the shade, they will need less water. Fertilize regularly for best flowering.

Money Plant
or Dollar Plant

(Lunaria annua)

Who wouldn't want to own something called the money plant? Especially when the silver, papery seedpods look just like heavenly coins? The fragrant purple and white flowers and arching branches with delicate seedpods have delighted children for centuries. They are easy to grow and simple to dry, and they look great in arrangements.

Projects

+ Cutting Gardens
+ Dried Flowers
+ Science Experiment Gardens—Seed Dispersal

Plant care

Sow seed in late fall or early spring. Money plants prefer partial shade and are very forgiving of soil. Decorative boughs can be cut and dried once seedpods develop.

27

Nasturtium

(Tropaeolum majus)

Common nasturtium is a great plant for children. The brightly colored orange, yellow, and red flowers are joyful and edible. The wide, almost rubbery leaves, though spicy, are also edible. Nasturtium's climbing, vining habit is a delight to watch over a summer season. Plant it where you can watch it grow and can snitch leaves and flowers for a peppery kick in your salad.

Plant care

Nasturtiums can be started from seed with a little effort, but they are easily bought as already started plants in early spring. They will tolerate full sun to a fair amount of shade, but they prefer sandy, poor soil. Do not fertilize. If they receive too many nutrients, they will not flower well.

Caution: Growers often coat nasturtium seeds. If eaten, the coating will cause nausea.

Projects

+ Edible Gardens
+ Five-Senses Container Gardens
+ Whimsy Gardens

© Ball Horticultural Company

Pansy and Viola

(Viola hybrids)

Pansies are a great plant for kids—they are edible, happy-faced, and easy to grow. The mound of rich, green foliage parts for a stem topped with cute flower faces in every shade from white, yellow, and orange, to blue, purple, and nearly black, with wonderful new combinations coming out all the time! Their cousins, Johnny jump ups, resemble miniature pansies with smaller, single flowers. Pansies and violas are fairly winter-hardy and can even last for multiple years, if planted in some shade and sheared back in the midsummer. Their happy faces last well into fall and then greet us in the spring.

Projects

+ Cutting Gardens
+ Edible Gardens
+ Holiday Projects— Spring Holidays and Fall Events
+ Native Plant Gardens
+ Rock Gardens

Plant care

Buy pansies and violas in the fall or early spring. Plant them directly into the ground in light shade and remove spent flowers for continued blooming.

29

Passionflower

(*Passiflora* hybrids)

Passionflower vine climbs by tendrils, wrapping around a support to rise toward the sun, and then flowers with big purple-blue rims around white to golden-yellow faces. The effect is magical, which is why passionflowers are so beloved. Floating in a bowl of water, it makes a lovely, though short-lived, cut flower. The ensuing seedpods can also be showy (and sometimes edible, depending on the variety). The juice of the edible varieties' fruit is delicious. Their real joy is as a summer, sun-loving vine covered with huge, slightly fragrant flowers in the mid to late summer.

Plant care

Buy passionflowers as rooted cuttings or already trellised plants. Plant them in full sun, and water and fertilize well through-out the growing season for best results. With some care, they can overwinter indoors.

Projects

+ Butterfly Gardens
+ Native Plant Gardens
+ Seashore Gardens
+ Whimsy Gardens

Petunia

(Petunia x *hybrida)*

We plant petunias because they are cheerful. The large, rounded, star-shaped flowers come in almost every color under the sun (there are even striped varieties!) and flower all summer long on dense, almost velvety foliage. What more could we ask of them? They are even fun to deadhead!

Projects

+ Hanging Baskets and Container Gardens
+ Plant a Rainbow
+ Seashore Gardens

Plant care

Petunias are not easy to grow from seed, so it is preferable to buy them as seedlings in flats from a garden center or grower. They need full sun and regular watering, though they must have good drainage and air circulation or they will rot. Fertilize once a month. Deadhead regularly to promote flowering.

31

Rose Moss

(Portulaca grandifora)

Rose moss just invites children to play with it! Thick, fleshy foliage ends in tiny, delicate, rose-like flowers. Available in a rainbow of colors with bright yellow stamens, this succulent-looking annual is one of kids' favorites for our hanging basket projects. It is pretty to look at and really fun to touch. It is also a great groundcover for poor soil areas and does beautifully at the shore.

Plant care

Rose moss requires well-drained soil. It tolerates drought and heat and does well at the seashore. The flowers open only in the sun. At night and on gray or cloudy days, they remain closed.

Projects

+ Hanging Baskets and Container Gardens
+ Plant a Rainbow
+ Rock Gardens
+ Seashore Gardens

Snapdragon

(Antirrhinum majus)

No child's garden is complete without snapdragons. The happy upright spires of tapering flowers are easy to grow and provide a great learning experience for kids. They come in nearly every color under the sun and range in size from dwarfs to tall, back-of-the-border plants. Kids love to make puppet faces with their "mouths." They are also excellent for cutting. If you continue to deadhead, they will rebloom until frost. Or if you cut the stalk way back after the first major bloom, they will grow another bloom stalk.

Projects

+ Cutting Gardens
+ Plant a Rainbow

Plant care

It is best to buy flats of snapdragons after the last frost. They prefer rich, well-drained, slightly basic (high pH) soil. If you have acidic soil, be sure to add some lime when planting. They need full sun and will tolerate heat. Keep them well watered, and deadhead or they will cease to bloom.

33

Spider Flower
(*Cleome* hybrids)

Light, airy spider flower dances on the breeze. It is especially lovely at dusk when the pastel pink, lavender, and white flowers glow in the fading light at the tops of their flexible stems, with their little foliage arms akimbo. Spider flower makes a nice cut flower and adds an airy elegance to the garden.

Plant care

Buy flats of spider flower at last frost. You can plant them into almost any soil, but they need full sun. They tolerate heat and drought well, and they will self-sow!

Projects

+ Butterfly Gardens
+ Cutting Gardens
+ Native Plant Gardens
+ Whimsy Gardens

Statice

(*Limonium sinuatum*)

There are few who won't recognize this classic dried flower. However, statice is easy and fun to grow as an annual and makes a great cut flower as well. Its flowers come in many other shades besides the very familiar purple, such as white, pink, blue, yellow, and lavender, and they sit above clumps of dark green foliage. Statice is a great start to a cutting or dried flower garden.

Projects

+ Cutting Gardens
+ Dried Flowers
+ Plant a Rainbow
+ Seashore Gardens

Plant care

It is best to buy statice already started in flats. It tolerates heat, drought, and full sun, but it needs loamy soil. So you need to mix in organics when planting. It also does well at the shore.

35

Strawflower

(Helichrysum bracteatum)

Strawflower is possibly the best dried flower, especially for children. It is easy to grow and easy to dry. It comes in brilliant colors from white to orange to purple, and the texture of the flowers feels "dry" even when it's fresh. The foliage is not much to look at, so strawflower is best grown in the cutting garden or mixed into a bed.

Plant care

Strawflowers grow best in full sun, well-drained soil, and hot conditions. Water them only as needed. You can grow them from seed sown directly onto the soil after the last frost or buy them in flats. Dwarf strawflower varieties can be used anywhere, but the taller varieties will need to be supported.

Projects

+ Dried Flowers
+ Plant a Rainbow
+ Seashore Gardens

36

Sweet Pea

(Lathyrus odoratus)

Sweet pea is a classic childhood favorite with delicate, fairy-like flowers in every color of the rainbow. It makes a wonderful cut flower and presses well, too. This climbing vine grows rapidly and by the end of the summer can attain quite a size and appearance. Newer cultivars have also reclaimed the famed sweet pea fragrance, so be sure you get a fragrant cultivar.

Projects

+ Cutting Gardens
+ Native Plant Gardens
+ Whimsy Gardens

Plant care

Sweet peas can be hard to grow from seed, so it is usually best to buy started plants. Plant them in early spring. Sweet peas do not tolerate hot, dry climates well. Plant where they can have sunny faces, but cool roots. Mulch the roots for added protection. Water and fertilize regularly. They need something to climb on, such as a trellis. They will flower until the heat of the summer and then fade away.

Caution: Eating the seeds of this plant can cause intestinal discomfort!

37

© Jill Dessauer

Sweet William

(Dianthus barbatus)

Sweet William makes a big spring show and then disappears with the summer heat. You will have a dense mat of profuse, lacy-edged flowers in shades of white to pink to purple and red in late spring. The plant then fades away before the heat of summer hits, leaving room for later annuals or perennials. With its clean, spicy fragrance and showy blooms, this dianthus is especially nice along the edge of a path or in a rock garden.

Plant care

Technically a biennial, dianthus is best bought in flats after the last frost. It prefers sun to light shade and slightly basic soil. If you deadhead, it will reflower for you, though it will still fade in the heat. It is a good reseeder!

Projects

+ Container Gardens
+ Rock Gardens

Caution: Some people experience an allergic reaction to the sap of this plant!

Verbena

(Verbena spp.)

As one of the most popular garden annuals, verbena comes in a variety of colors from red, white, and blue to pinks and lavenders—all of them are festive and many have a white "eye" in the center. They come in a range of growing habits and include some good trailing varieties for hanging baskets. They are the perfect pick-me-up for any hot, dry spot.

Projects

+ Hanging Baskets
+ Butterfly Gardens
+ Native Plant Gardens
+ Plant a Rainbow
+ Seashore Gardens

Plant care

Tricky to start from seed, verbena is best bought already started just after the last frost. It needs good air circulation. Fertilize it at a low dosage throughout the growing season.

39

Zinnia
(*Zinnia* spp.)

Zinnias are a must-have for a children's garden. They are happy plants in the garden, as cut flowers, and in containers. The single and double pompom faces come in every color except blue, and more are available every year. Their large, lush green foliage makes a nice backdrop for the vivid colors. They do well in cutting gardens as well as in beds, borders, and containers. No home should be without zinnias!

Plant care

Zinnias start easily from seed. They do well in hot, dry areas with good air circulation. They need full sun. Water only their roots. If the foliage or flowers stay wet, they may develop fungus. Deadhead the plants for continued flowering.

Projects

+ Container Gardens
+ Butterfly Gardens
+ Cutting Gardens
+ Native Plant Gardens
+ Plant a Rainbow
+ Seashore Gardens
+ Whimsy Gardens

When the garden outside is hiding underground, a houseplant is a great friend to have.

Chapter 4

Easy Exotics and Indoor Plants

When thinking of gardening, most people overlook one of the most rewarding gardens—an indoor one. Houseplants stay with us through the winter and often flower all year long. African violets rarely take a break, bromeliad flowers last for months, and spider plants throw pups at any time of year. When the garden outside is hiding underground, a houseplant is a great friend to have. Here are a few that are fun and easy.

African Violet

(*Saintpaulia* hybrids)

African violets are the one of the most popular houseplants and for good reason—they are easy to grow, do not require full sun, take up little space, and flower almost year round. The flowers come in a wide variety of shapes and colors, from singles to multi-flowers, and from white, pink, and red to blue and purple. African violets are also easy to propagate. They are a welcome gift and great fun to receive!

Plant care

Bright, indirect sunlight is best. Water when the soil surface has just begun to dry with warm water. Water African violets from the bottom—into the saucer or at the rim of the container. Do not soak the crown of the plant. Drainage should be excellent. Never leave water sitting in the saucer. Fertilize once a month with a water-soluble solution. (There are many formulations specifically for African violets) Turn plants occasionally, as they will grow toward the sun. Put them outside in a shady location during warm, summer months if possible. To propagate, break off an inner leaf, and root it either in loose potting soil or in darkened water, and then plant into soil when roots have grown (in fourteen to twenty-one days).

41

Bromeliad

(Bromeliaceae family)

There are many, many different kinds of bromeliads, including pineapples. The one thing they all share in common is tiny scales that serve as a very efficient absorption system. In species found in desert regions, these scales help the plant to reduce water loss and shield the plants from solar radiation. Bromeliads are champions at conserving water. But in the end, bromeliads are cool to look at and fun to grow. My favorite kinds form funnels in which water collects and then is stored for the plants' use. They have big, stiff leaves, sometimes in multi-colors, and tall spiky flowers that last for months. Bromeliads are relatively maintenance free and have striking flowers. Try one!

Project

+ Science Experiment
  Gardens—
  Propagation

Plant care

Purchase bromeliads in the greenhouse section of a good garden center. Generally they will be in flower when sold. When the flower dies back (after several months), the stalk will gradually die afterward. Before the flower dies, the plant will produce offsets, called pups, around its base. To make more bromeliads, separate the pups from the main plant when the pups are a third to half the size of the "mother plant" and plant them in a new pot.

Caution: Some bromeliads have spiky leaves.

Chenille Plant

(Echevaria leucotricha)

This Mexican native delights children, who cannot resist touching the fuzzy, pink-to-red flowers that hang down. It makes a great houseplant and is best hung by a sunny window, where you can enjoy the look of the fleshy leaves and touch the fuzzy flowers whenever you get the urge.

Plant care

Buy as a houseplant. Keep where very warm, 65 to 80° preferred. Keep evenly moist, but not sitting in water. Chenille plants prefer morning sun, bright light in the spring and summer months, and full sun in the fall and winter months.

43

Flowering Maple

(Abutilon hybrids)

Flowering maple is a wonderful houseplant with large, lobed leaves and fantastic, drooping yellow, orange, pink, or red flowers. The colorful flowers resemble unfurling lanterns or bells, and new colors are introduced all the time! The variegated varieties are particularly pretty. Flowering maples can be used as annuals for special places, or displayed outside for the summer and then brought in for the winter.

Plant care

These are hard to find, but you can purchase them at greenhouses, at garden centers, or online. Keep them in a container in a mostly sunny location. Keep them well watered but not in standing water. Repot every few years, adding organics when you do.

Project

+ Container Gardens

Ice Plant, Hottentot Fig, or Highway Ice Plant

(Carpobrotus edulis)

Projects

+ Five-Senses Container Gardens

+ Rock Gardens

This is the very cool plant you see growing along the highways of Southern California. With proper care, it can make a really fun houseplant, annual, or in warmer locations yard plant. (A word of caution: In the right climate, it can become invasive.) The fruits and even the seeds are edible. Flowers are white, pink, and purple and have a slight fragrance. The foliage is triangular, succulent, and sensory.

Plant care

Purchase ice plants in the greenhouse section of a good garden center or online. They need full sun and well-drained soil. It is best to plant them into very sandy soil in a pot with good drainage holes. Water sparingly.

45

Jade Plant

(Crassula argentea)

The large-growing, succulent jade plant features rich green, rubbery leaves and lots of tiny, white flowers. You can propagate them by breaking off a leaf and pushing the cut side into soil. The leaf will root and form a new plant. I received one in a dish garden when I was eleven years old and still have a piece of it, despite overwatering, over-sunning, and nearly freezing it twice.

Plant care

Purchase jade plants in the greenhouse section of a good garden center or online. They need full sun and well-drained soil. It is best to plant into very sandy soil in a pot with good drainage holes. Water sparingly. Break off leaves at the stem, leave them for a day or two, and then plant them into good potting soil. In about a month you will see the plant has rooted and is making new little leaves. So cool!

© Ellen Zachos

46

Lipstick Plant

(Aeschynanthus radicans)

Lipstick plant is one of the funniest looking plants you will see. The leaves are fleshy and green, reddish, or variegated. Its flowers are bright red to orange and look as if they are twisting up out of lipstick tubes on cascading branches. This cheerful plant brightens up the house!

Plant care

Lipstick plants are generally sold in greenhouses. They prefer bright light, but not full sun. They like well-drained soil. *Do not* let water sit in the container.

47

Living Rocks

(*Lithops* spp. and *Pleiospilos* spp.)

These fun, little succulents look just like the rocks they grow near. They are short and compact, with flat or slightly rounded tops. They slowly "break open" at the center as new leaves form. They will live quietly in sunny windows with almost no care.

Plant care

Living rocks can be found in most garden centers or online. Plant them into very sandy soil, and place in a sunny window where temperatures do not fall below 55 to 60°. Every month or two, water them. Do not leave water standing in the container.

Pink Polka Dot Plant

(Hypoestes phyllostachya)

Pink polka dot plant is a truly joyful houseplant or annual. It has leaves that are literally dotted with pink polka dots. (Some new varieties have red or white dots.) Use it as a houseplant, or plant several in an annual bed or in a partly sunny spot that needs brightening up. You will feel happier every time you look at them!

Project

+ Rainbow Gardens
+ Whimsy Gardens

Plant care

Polka dot plants need bright light but not full sun, and slightly moist, rich soil. They tend to get leggy, so pinch them back as needed.

49

Spider Plant

(Chlorophytum comosum)

The easily recognizable spider plant is one of the most popular houseplants. Its long, green or variegated, strap-like leaves and arching stalks with "pups" forming at the ends that resemble a spider. Spider plants are a great way to teach kids how to propagate. Each little hanging pup can be cut off and rooted in water or soil to start a new plant, which can then be given as a gift or kept to eventually overrun the house.

Plant care

Someone, somewhere has a spider plant pup they are longing to give you. Spider plants will tolerate very wet feet and benign neglect, and they will create pups no matter what you do to stop them, which we often feel we must plant, making even more plants. They are virtually indestructible. The variegated form needs more sun than the solid green, which will tolerate a fair amount of shade. Children love them. They are a great first indoor plant.

Project

+ Science Experiment Gardens— Propagation

Venus Flytrap

(*Dionaea muscipula*)

There is something about a plant that can eat animals that appeals to the savage inside all of us. Venus flytraps have adapted to living tucked into tree branches high above the ground, where their access to nutrients is zero. By catching small insects and absorbing their body fluids, the plants are able to get the minerals they need.

Project

+ Native Plant Gardens

This is both a wonderful example of how flora and fauna adapt to their environments as well as the factual inspiration needed for most children's imaginations to run wild. The plant's wild, "toothed" look thrills kids, as does the way the mouths snap shut when touched. Venus flytraps must be kept in humid terrariums, but they spark something primal in kids (and adults), who cannot get enough of them!

Plant care

Venus flytraps can be found in most garden centers. Pick one with good, rich color and more than one mouth. They do best in a large, wide-mouthed container, with a bottom layer of charcoal topped with a layer of sphagnum or peat moss. They need to stay humid, but without soaking. Keep the charcoal layer moist, but not saturated. Venus flytraps need light but not direct sun (otherwise they will bake inside their container.) Ideally, they need only one mouth fed every three to four weeks. They are tricky, but with proper care, they can live for years.

51

Zebra Plant

(Aphelandra squarrosa)

This native of South America is just plain fun! White veins highlight dramatic, long, dark, glossy-green leaves on this showy, upright plant. Multidimensional yellow spikes of flowers appear in midsummer. The plant looks prehistoric and is fun to have around the house.

Plant care

Bright, indirect sunlight is best for zebra plants. Water when the soil surface has just begun to dry. Water less in winter and just after flowering. Zebra plants drop leaves if over- or under-watered and prefer high humidity.

Water gardens can be as simple as a water lily in a tub or as complex as a built-in pond with a waterfall.

Chapter 5

Grow
a Pond

Water gardens can be as simple as a water lily in a tub or as complex as a built-in pond with a waterfall. A full-fledged water garden is something to plan carefully, as you want it to be safe for the children who visit it. But the effort is rewarded in the joy kids get from water, and the flora and fauna found there. Even if your garden is only a bucket with some water-loving plants and a few goldfish, you will be amazed at how children are drawn to it with endless questions. For a more complex garden, I strongly suggest you schedule a consultation with a reputable garden designer, or that you do a lot of research into pond designing and building. Before planting any water garden, do some serious research to match the right plants to your water garden's capacity and environment. Some plants can be "plunked" into a cache pot or barrel of water relatively easily and give great satisfaction to your budding gardeners, while others require more space and care.

Lotus

(Nelumbo spp.)

Lotuses are exquisite plants and surprisingly hardy. They are not for everyone, however. You must have a nice-sized pool for a lotus. The leaves are huge, spreading out in the water and acting as shelter and anchor for the growing flowers, which tower over the leaves on tall, sturdy stems. The pods that linger after the flowers can be dried and used as rattles or in flower arrangements. Lotuses need a lot of space, but their flowers, seedpods, and overall beauty make them a must-have for any serious water gardener. Though lotuses are usually thought of as coming from Asia, Nelumbo lutea are native to North America.

Projects

+ Native Plant
  Gardens
+ Water Gardens

Plant care

You will need to do some serious research to match the right lotus plant with your water garden's space and climate. But lotuses are so fascinating to children, they are worth the extra time and effort! Lotuses are also a great starting point for stories about Asia and Eastern culture.

53

© Ellen Zachos

Water Hyacinth

(Eichhornia crassipes)

Though not recommended for release into the wild, water hyacinths still make a great beginner water garden plant for kids. The big, juicy-looking leaves float, so the plant bobs around the water, while spikes of lavender flowers stand up like buoys. New pups grow off the original plant, forming colonies that can become invasive in warmer climates. In a controlled home garden, however, they are just fun to watch. Water hyacinth is hardy to about Zone 8.

Project

+ Water Gardens

Plant care

Purchase water hyacinth at any water gardening Web site or store. Use in contained water gardens or barrels. This plant will spread rapidly and can be divided easily. Do not release water hyacinth into native water, as it is invasive.

Water Lily

(Nymphaea spp.)

Water lilies take a more lasting commitment than most plants, but they are worth it. The beauty of the round, rubbery, green leaves floating on the water and the delicate, cup-shaped flowers make this one of the most beautiful flowers in any garden. Water lily flowers come in a huge range of day and night bloomers and in a rainbow of colors from white and yellow to deep red and purple. Some varieties are winter hardy (in deeper water), while some are tropical and must be brought in for the winter. Water lilies can be planted alone in large tubs or containers, without requiring an entire water garden and filtration system to support them. You can even enjoy these tropical lilies outside in the summer and bring them inside in fishbowls in the winter (as they have been doing for hundreds of years in China). Nothing seems to appeal to kids more than to see a flower rising up out of the water and to play with drops of water on giant leaves.

Projects

+ Native Plant Gardens
+ Water Gardens

Plant care

Most water gardening supply stores will have both tropical and hardy water lilies. Be prepared for your purchase by knowing your garden's water depth and if the water lily will be left outside or be brought in for winter. Ask whether the plant is a day or night bloomer and what its hardiness is. Then bring it home, plunk it into the water, and enjoy. Water lilies usually prefer full sun and still water, so place them away from flowing water and fountains.

Chapter 6

Herbs and Veggies

Culinary Crops

Herbs and vegetables are a great way to garden with children. Starting seeds inside is a nice jump on spring, and shopping for baby plants to bring home to the garden is a great way to bond with your kids. The plants are fun to watch grow, but it is even more fun to pick fresh produce off the stem and eat. Best of all, kids who have seen the cycle from seed to edible plant develop an appreciation for what it takes to get food to the table, especially if they are able to make the contribution from the "fruits" of their own labor. Here are a few that are relatively easy to grow with good results. (Also, don't forget radishes, which are included in chapter 1 on page 7.)

55

Basil

(Ocimun basilicum)

Basil is a great annual herb to grow with other vegetables. It is easy to grow from seed, or to buy and pop in around the garden or in containers. The tall, bushy plants grow bushier as you pick the top growth to eat. There are purple- or green-colored and curly- or solid-leaved varieties. Basil is beautiful to look at, easy to grow, and smells delicious! Best of all, fresh basil is easy to incorporate into recipes, and children love the satisfaction of picking something to bring to the table to eat.

Projects

+ Five-Senses Container Gardens

+ Science Experiment Gardens—Seed Exploration

+ Vegetable Gardens

Plant care

Plant seeds directly into the soil or container after the last frost. They need full sun and well-drained soil. Basil will germinate within the week, sending up more and more aromatic leaves on thick, square stems. Pinch out the top growth to force the plant to stay shorter and bushier. Pinch out the flower stalks as soon as you see them, as the leaves get bitter once the plant flowers. Pinch leaves straight off the stem, rinse them, pat them dry, then serve them with fresh tomato and mozzarella, or incorporate chopped or torn leaves into your cooking.

56

Carrot

(Daucus carota var. *sativa)*

The carrots we eat are actually the root of the carrot plant. The seeds sprout delicate ferny leaves as they push their orange bodies deep into the soil and fatten underground. When it is time to harvest (the foliage will start to wilt and brown), simply pull the roots up by the foliage. But be careful to look for feeding caterpillars first. Carrot leaves are a favorite of many of the butterfly larvae we want to keep around!

Plant care

Carrots are annuals. Because they have to muscle their way down into the soil in a short time frame, carrots prefer loose, sandy soil. They also prefer cool weather. They will tolerate a little shade, but you should try to plant them into the coolest, yet sunny part of the garden. Add lots of sand if the soil is heavy and do not add compost or manure. The seeds are tiny, so you will end up planting a lot. When they sprout, thin them out, so each little root will have room to grow. When the foliage starts to flop over, that's a good sign that the carrots are ready to eat.

Projects

+ Butterfly Gardens
+ Native Plant Gardens
+ Science Experiment Gardens— Seed Exploration
+ Vegetable Gardens

Corn

(Zea mays var. *rugosa)*

If you have the room, corn is a lot of fun to grow and nothing tastes better than corn fresh from the garden. But you must have room for at least sixteen plants for the best pollination, so be prepared. Corn is a wonderful imagination grower for kids. Plant it early, and then watch it grow taller than the kids, making great walls for forts or mazes ("maizes") or acting as support for other climbing vegetables. Best of all is when kids can go into the garden and pick their very own. No one will complain about eating their vegetables once they have eaten corn fresh from the garden!

Projects

+ Native Plant Gardens
+ Science Experiment Gardens—Seed Exploration
+ Vegetable Gardens
+ Whimsy Gardens

Plant care

Corn can be sown directly into the soil after the last frost; sown inside a few weeks before frost then transplanted outside; or bought already started. Prepare the soil well with lots of compost and composted manure before you plant, because corn uses a lot of nutrients from the soil. Give each plant lots of room, but plant them in a square, not a row, as corn is pollinated by the wind. (A square of four plants by four plants or five by five will give you a nice crop of corn). Be sure to water well on the soil only, and watch carefully for bugs. Harvest when the silk begins to brown, and then use the cornstalks for fall decorations. Plant corn in a different part of the garden each year, or add lots of organics when replanting this annual in the same spot, as it depletes the nutrients from the soil.

58

Cucumber

(Cucumis sativas)

Cucumbers grow on trailing vines, which can be trained up a trellis or left to wander. They sprout quickly from seed and begin to vine almost immediately. Small, yellow flowers appear soon, followed by "cukes," anywhere from fifty-five to seventy days after seed was sown. Most kids like to eat fresh cucumbers, but even if they don't, they will enjoy watching the plants snake across the garden.

Plant care

These annuals are easy to grow from seed. Sow cucumber seed just after the last frost into soil that has been enriched with compost or composted manure, in a sunny, warm spot in the garden. Provide long, deep drinks of water often. Harvest when the cucumbers are firm, green, and not too large, or they will get bitter.

Projects

+ Science Experiment Gardens—Seed Exploration
+ Vegetable Gardens

Dill

(Anethum graveolens)

This tall, ferny, annual herb looks lovely in the garden. It is also a wonderful flavor to add to a salad or summer meal, and the large, windmill-like seed heads can be dried and the seeds harvested for yearlong cooking. Even better, it is a favorite of many of the caterpillars who will turn into butterflies, so dill is a versatile and cherished addition to most gardens.

Projects

+ Butterfly Gardens
+ Cutting Gardens
+ Science Experiment Gardens—Seed Exploration
+ Vegetable Gardens

Plant care

Dill will germinate well in the cool weeks before the last frost, so sow seed directly into the garden. They have a long, thin taproot and will grow to three feet, so plant into loose, organic soil, and plant close together, or against a fence for support. (Place them at the back of your garden bed.) Before you pluck off the caterpillars you will find on them in mid to late summer, be sure that you are not discarding growing monarch butterflies. Dill is one of their favorites. If you don't harvest the seeds, you will find dill will reseed from year to year, showing up in new parts of the garden.

60

Green Bean

(Phaseolus vulgaris)

Green beans are an easy, delicious way for children to begin a vegetable garden. These cute annuals are easy to grow. Beans can be pole or bush, meaning either they will vine up a support or form a small, spreading plant. They will bear beans in anywhere from forty to seventy days from first being sown, which is a short enough timeframe for children to stay interested.

The beans hang tucked into the foliage, so kids have fun searching for beans for dinner. Because fresh beans off the vine are so delicious, they may never make it to the table!

Projects

+ Native Plant Gardens

+ Science Experiment Gardens— Propagation

+ Vegetable Gardens

Plant care

Sow seeds indoors two to three weeks before the last frost, and then transplant the seedlings outside in a sunny location safe from strong winds. Or purchase as seedlings around the last frost and plant directly into the ground. Plant into rich, well-drained soil. Water deeply once or twice per week. Stake or trellis pole beans, or make a teepee of the poles for a great garden hideaway. Plant two to three patches a week apart for longer harvest.

Lettuce

(Lactuca sativa)

Lettuce is one of my favorite edible annuals to plant with kids. The seeds are cute and easy to sow. The plants germinate quickly. Head lettuce must be left until the head is ready for harvesting, but there are wonderful new varieties, like the mesclun mixes, with fantastic colors, uniquely shaped leaves, and distinctive flavors, making eating lettuce a sensory delight! Once there are at least six leaves on a plant, you can pinch off leaves as you walk by, nibbling on their delicious freshness.

Projects

+ Container Gardens
+ Holiday Projects— Fall Events
+ Native Plant Gardens
+ Science Experiment Gardens—Seed Exploration
+ Vegetable Gardens

Plant care

Plant into rich, well-drained soil, in bright light but not full sun. Lettuce is a cool-weather crop and is best planted a few weeks before the last frost and then again just as the weather begins to cool. It germinates quickly so you will enjoy two crops, avoiding the heat of the summer in the middle. Keep evenly moist but not too wet, because overwatered lettuce will rot. Harvest one out of every three leaves once it has at least six leaves, then continue to harvest until it "bolts" (i.e., sends up a seed stalk), at which point the leaves will get bitter.

62

Mint

(Mentha spicata)

Mint is an invasive perennial, but it's the one plant I cannot do without in the garden. The plants are rich green with delicate flowers on tall, square stems. They spread by runners and must be contained to avoid overrunning their space. Field mint is native to North America and has been used for centuries to flavor food and soothe the body and spirit. A pinched leaf or two into the mouth or in a cool glass of tea on a hot day is an instant refresher.

Plant care

Purchase plants already started. Plant into a space where they are either contained or can spread without it being a problem. They prefer full sun but will tolerate a little shade, and they like rich, moist soil. I like to point out to kids that the stems are square. It doesn't mean anything, it's just a cool fact!

Projects

+ Container Gardens
+ Cutting Gardens
+ Edible Gardens
+ Five-Senses Container Gardens
+ Native Plant Gardens
+ Science Experiment Gardens—Seed Exploration
+ Seashore Gardens
+ Vegetable Gardens

63

Parsley
(Petroselinum crispum)

Have you ever really looked at parsley? It is a beautiful plant and makes a great leafy-green accent in a planter. Its fresh, clean scent and rich green, finely dissected leaves make it nice to have in flower containers or in the garden. Parsley is also a great "snip and snack" plant. I plant parsley where I can see it, but also where I can reach it when I am cooking or garnishing. It is also a very hardy annual!

Projects

+ Container Gardens
+ Butterfly Gardens
+ Five-Senses Container Gardens
+ Vegetable Gardens

Plant care

Parsley can be tricky to germinate, so buy already started plants and transplant them into containers or the garden. They need full sun and well-drained soil. Do not let them dry out between waterings, or the plants will decline due to damaged roots. When harvesting, use sharp scissors and snip parsley stalks close to the ground, to stimulate more growth.

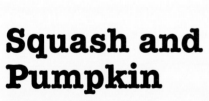

© Ellen Zachos

Squash and Pumpkin

(Cucurbita spp.)

Squash and pumpkins are native to North America and have been grown here for centuries. (Pumpkins are a part of the larger squash family. They have differences but the same growing requirements.) There is something wonderful about growing squash in the garden—the vines are long and tendrilly, the flowers are big and yellow, and the leaves are huge and hide the growing fruit. The fruit itself, when it grows, is a delight to watch. But beware—squash take up a lot of room!

Plant care

One to two squash plants will take up a big part of your garden. Plant the seeds (or already started plants) into raised mounds of soil and compost in a sunny spot. Keep the plants well watered. Squash have male and female flowers on the same plant, pollinated by insects, but only the female flowers bear fruit. The Native American plant combination called the three sisters is a good way to grow squash in the garden (see page 145 for more). When touching pumpkins, be careful! The stems of the pumpkins are covered with tiny spines. You should wear gloves when handling pumpkins. If you want "perfect" pumpkins, make a little stand from a tuna can or a piece of wood or bricks, to rest the bottom of the pumpkin off the ground. This way the fruit will form without marks on the bottom side. When the fruit turns color and "thumps" hollow, it is just about ripe.

> ## Projects
> + Science Experiment Gardens—Seed Exploration
> + Vegetable Gardens

Thyme

(Thymus vulgaris)

Thyme may not seem like a plant for children at first glance, but watch them play on a pathway interplanted with thyme and you will change your mind. Thyme is a low-growing, perennial groundcover, with a rich, evocative scent and delicate white to purple flowers. It can be picked for the kitchen or walked on with bare feet for pure sensory bliss.

Projects

+ Cutting Gardens
+ Five-Senses Container Gardens
+ Rock Gardens
+ Shady Hideaway Gardens
+ Vegetable Gardens

Plant care

Thyme can be bought as seed and sown easily, or specific cultivars can be bought and planted in mid-spring. It is a perennial and will spread a little each year. Thyme likes full sun to partial shade, hot climates, and well-drained soil. Snip fresh growth in the early morning for the best flavor for cooking.

66

Tomato
(Lycopersicon lycopersicum)

Tomatoes can be planted in containers or directly into the garden. They are upright, bushy plants that grow considerably throughout the season and require plenty of space and usually staking. The tiny, yellow flowers will give way to fruit that will take a while to form, and then suddenly give you more fruit than you can use at one time. There are many kinds of tomatoes, so plan on having more than one. In my garden each year, I like to plant a big slicing tomato, cherry or grape tomatoes, and one or two different varieties, such as a Roma or an unusual heirloom variety. I try to plan for varied harvest times and almost never manage. But do not get carried away—three to five plants are enough to last you all season! Of course, if you have too much, you can always share them with friends or family; blanch and freeze them; make spaghetti sauce, fresh salsa, or chili; or donate them to a local food pantry.

Projects

+ Science Experiment Gardens—Seed Exploration
+ Vegetable Gardens

Plant care

Tomatoes need warm soil, full sun, warm nights, lots of organic material, and even moisture. You can sow seeds indoors three to five weeks before the last frost to give the plants a head start, and them move them outside after the last chance of frost to a sunny, sheltered location. Or you can buy them already started. Add lots of compost or composted manure when planting. Tomatoes take a lot of nutrients out of the soil, so the more they start with, the happier they will be. Be sure to plant them a little deeper than most plants.

Culinary Crops

Fruit

Fruits are a wonderful addition to your vegetable or edible garden. Watermelons are an easy annual and can go in a *big* corner of your garden. (They take a lot of space, sun, water, and nutrients!) Due to their plant size, berry shrubs and fruit trees take more initial thought and care when choosing where to plant them. But once they are in the ground and established, you will have fruit for years to come. There is something wonderful and homey about plants that give you fruit each year. It is the stuff of childhood memories!

67

Apple
(*Malus* spp.)

American history is full of stories about apple trees. I am a firm believer that every child-hood should have at least one. Apples are great climbing trees as well as good hide-and-seek trees. The fruit is great for pies and jams, healthy snacks, and lessons on where food comes from. Picking apples in the fall and eating them ties a person to nature.

You can cut a few branches in the winter to bring inside to force the blooms and have a touch of spring in the middle of winter. An apple tree in the backyard is also nice to read under. The tree itself will grow rounded and bushy. Once it is six to ten years old, it will begin to flower (see picture) and fruit. As the tree gets older, it will fruit more and more, often in a "one year heavy, one year light" pattern. Some trees are self-pollinating, while some need another apple tree to pollinate well.

Projects

+ Edible Gardens
+ Native Plant Gardens
+ Seashore Gardens

Plant care

Find a variety that is self-pollinating, or be sure you have at least two trees. Add lots of organics when you plant, and locate the tree in a full-sun spot, where it has room to grow. Water deeply at least once a week. Your tree may take a few years before it bears fruit, depending on how large it is when you buy it.

Caution: All parts of this plant except the fruit are poisonous. Even the seeds contain cyanide. In large doses, they can cause discomfort (though consuming large doses of apples will, too). Children should eat only the fruit and as few seeds as possible.

Blueberry

(Vaccinium corymbosum)

Blueberries are one of the best-kept secrets of the garden. They are upright shrubs that reach up to 6 feet tall and 8 to 10 feet wide over their long lives. Blueberries are easy to grow and produce delicious berries, almost no matter what you do to them. The stems are a beautiful red color in winter, and the fall foliage color is stunning. Kids love combing the shrub for ripe berries each summer morning. If you plant enough blueberries, there will be plenty for you and the attending wildlife, who will provide hours of entertainment.

Projects

+ Edible Gardens
+ Holiday Projects—
  Summer Events
+ Native Plant
  Gardens
+ Seashore Gardens

Plant care

Blueberries need very moist soil and will even do well in problematically wet spots. They need acidic soil and prefer full sun to partial shade. For good fruiting, plant at least two plants of different cultivars. The tiny, white flowers in spring are pretty, followed by the blueberries we all love in summer. Prune after fruiting.

69

Raspberry

(Rubus spp.)

Raspberries have thorns and can become invasive, so they are not for everyone. But I have found they so thrill the children I know that I have to include them. There seems to be nothing more delightful to some children than beating back a thorny shrub and emerging, scratched and bruised, with luscious berries (or the memory of popping them fresh off the vine into hungry mouths with the stained fingers and clothes to prove it happened). Gardening gloves and long sleeves are highly recommended when harvesting these kid-pleasing berries. They are long-lived shrubs, with small, slightly fragrant flowers in spring and delicious berries in midsummer.

Projects

+ Edible Gardens
+ Holiday Projects—Summer Events
+ Native Plant Gardens

Plant care

Raspberry shrubs can grow 6 feet tall and wide. There are two varieties: single fruiting and ever bearing. The former will fruit once each year, while the latter will fruit once, rest for a few weeks, and then give a second harvest. Both send up new canes each year, fruit on the cane in the second year, and then die. So each year you will have new growth, fruit on last year's growth, and old canes that will need to be pruned out. When planting raspberries, buy local varieties and plant into well-enriched soil in full sun or light shade. If possible, plant against a chain-link fence or other support that they can be trained to. This makes harvesting and maintaining much, much easier. Also plant where you can contain them, and vigorously prune out any canes that grow outside the area you have given them.

Strawberry

(Fragaria spp.)

Strawberries are a delicious fruit. What you may not know is that they are also a lovely plant for the garden. The delicate, white flowers are slightly fragrant, and the fruit forms tucked into the foliage. Strawberries, a perennial groundcover, are native to North America, but what most of us grow now is a hybrid of North and South American natives.

There are hybrids well suited for growing in any part of the United States, but no hybrid will do well everywhere, and there are both single-fruiting and ever-bearing varieties, so check your local sources for the best ones for your garden.

Plant care

Plant commercially grown plants in the early spring into rich, organic soil. Spread the roots out when planting, or the resulting plant will not grow as hardily. Keep the crown of the plant above the soil level when planting. Give each plant about one foot square, more if it is a variety that sends out profuse runners. Water deeply to promote root growth. Harvest the berries when they are full and at least 75% red. Strawberries can be planted into planters, like terraced pyramids or strawberry pots, to promote good air circulation and plant growth. These are great fun for kids, who have surprising patience for watering and picking over the plants for ripe berries.

Projects

+ Container Gardens
+ Edible Gardens
+ Holiday Projects—
  Summer Events
+ Native Plant
  Gardens

71

Watermelon
(*Citrullus lanatus*)

This tendrilling, annual vine can and will take over the yard by the end of the season. But since the end result will be big, fat melons, it is hard to be angry. The leaves are huge, the flowers goofy looking, and the fruit, as it forms, is almost cartoonish. I have never seen a child prouder than a small girl who grew a big watermelon and was preparing to share it with her family.

Plant care

Give this plant a lot of space. Dig a large hole in the warmest spot in the garden, one with full sun and good air circulation. Mix in lots of organics and sand to make a light, organic soil. In the South, plants can be started from seed; but in the North, with its shorter growing season, it is best to transplant store-bought seedlings a week or two after the last frost. Keep plants well watered. Melons are ripe when they sound "thick" or muffled when thumped, as opposed to hollow. Clean up the vine and compost at the end of the season to prevent overwintering bugs from staying in the garden.

Project

+ Edible Gardens

Perennials come back
year after year.

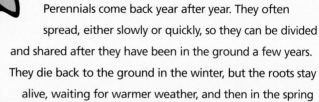

Perennials for Any Garden

Perennials come back year after year. They often spread, either slowly or quickly, so they can be divided and shared after they have been in the ground a few years. They die back to the ground in the winter, but the roots stay alive, waiting for warmer weather, and then in the spring they pop back up. Because they know they will survive, perennials are not as concerned about making seeds. This means they will not flower for as long as annuals do. Their bloom time is shorter, but they usually have interesting foliage. Plant layers of perennials in your garden, planning for flowers at different times and at varying heights, and then fill in with annuals. You will have a garden that changes from spring to fall and never looks dull. If you want to peek into the mind of a child, ask one to help you plan a perennial garden. You will be amazed at how easily children grasp these concepts and their retention of flower names, colors, and bloom times. Ask them to start garden journals, and you will find yourself spelling Latin names, identifying bugs, and explaining how the angle of the sun causes leaves and flowers to move. A perennial garden can be changed every year or last for centuries. Perennials teach that no matter how grim times get, life will reappear. It is a reassuring lesson for children of all ages.

Balloon Flower

(Platycodon grandiflorus)

Balloon flowers are a nearly perfect plant for kids—and everyone else! White, pink, and blue "balloons" form and pop open to star-shaped flowers, starting in late June and lasting into August. The stems are tall and graceful, with soft mounds of foliage at the base. Balloon flowers make wonderful cut flowers and lovely flower borders. The dwarf varieties are perfect for containers and rock gardens.

Projects

+ Container Gardens
+ Cutting Gardens
+ Rock Gardens

Plant care

Balloon flowers are carefree, long-lived garden plants. They need fairly full sun but can tolerate a little shade. They prefer good, rich, well-drained soil. The taller varieties may need staking, but the dwarf forms do not. They are late to emerge in spring, so be careful not to uproot or plant over them.

73

Bee Balm

(Monarda didyma)

Not only bees love this plant. Hummingbirds, butterflies, and humans cannot seem to stay away either. Maybe that's because bee balm is such a character: The flowers look like cartoon mop heads and come in a profusion of colors. The leaves smell like mint. The plant itself is a tough, carefree perennial, a great workhorse in the garden, a lovely addition to a flower border, and a wonderful cut flower. There are even dwarf varieties for smaller spaces.

Plant care

Bee balm prefers good, rich, well-drained soil and full sun to partial shade. Be careful: Bee balm can become invasive. Do not fertilize unless you want it to really take off. Divide every few years when the clump has grown wide and the center has died out. Then plant only the vigorous outer portions.

Projects

+ Container Gardens
+ Butterfly Gardens
+ Cutting Gardens
+ Seashore Gardens

Black-Eyed Susan

(Rudbeckia fulgida)

A six-year-old gardener once invited me to see her special garden patch, a small square completely overrun with black-eyed Susans and purple coneflowers. She thought it was the most wonderful place on Earth, and watching her weave among the stems, telling me about all of her adventures there, I had to agree with her.

Black-eyed Susan, a North American native, is no longer exclusively tall, yellow, and gangly. Many attractive dwarf and multi-colored varieties are on the market. But no sunny border is complete without them!

Projects

+ Butterfly Gardens
+ Cutting Gardens
+ Native Plant Gardens
+ Seashore Gardens
+ Whimsy Gardens

Plant care

Black-eyed Susans need full sun and moist, well-drained soil. They are incredibly tough. There are great new cultivars, so get to know them before you make a choice.

75

Daylily
(*Hemerocallis* hybrids)

Daylilies have come a long, long way from the wild tiger lilies I used to pick to make salads for my dolls. Even then I knew they were edible, and though I was not brave enough to pop one in my mouth, I fed them to my dolls every chance I got. Now there are literally thousands of named varieties (including 'Cinderella's Dark Side', a personal favorite), in colors from white to almost black and every possible hue in between. There are dwarves and tall, leggy giants for the back of borders. Each flower still only lasts one day, hence the name, though new varieties are profuse bloomers. The fried, fresh flowers are a delicacy, and the fleeting nature of their bloom makes them precious in the garden.

Projects

+ Butterfly Gardens
+ Cutting Gardens
+ Edible Gardens
+ Seashore Gardens

Plant care

Find a flower and habit you like, and then buy that variety. There are thousands of cultivated varieties. Daylilies prefer well-drained soil and full sun to light shade. Depending on the variety, they can bloom any time from May to September, or all summer, like 'Stella Dora' or 'Happy Returns' (another personal favorite). Remove faded flowers before seedpods form for continued bloom.

76

Ferns

There are hundreds of varieties of ferns, each with their own qualities and characteristics. For a shady, moist spot, ferns are an ideal plant. With their fronds and seedpods, ferns make a wonderful addition to any child's garden. Fern fronds make excellent wands, fans, "feathers," and costumes. They come in shades from deepest, richest green to almost golden yellow, with many variegations and colorations in between. With adult guidance, fiddleheads may be picked and eaten. Here are a few of my favorites ferns:

- Maidenhair fern (*Adiantum pedatum*)—Grows 1 to 2 feet high and wide, with delicate, light green, fan-shaped fronds. It features a great gold, autumn color and is wonderful around trees. Do not overwater!
- Japanese painted fern (*Athyrium nipponicum* 'Pictum')—The 1- to 2-foot clumps have green foliage with a silvery metallic sheen on the topsides with burgundy red stems.
- Ostrich fern or fiddlehead fern (*Matteuccia struthiopteris*)—The 3- to 4-foot clumps feature upright, arching, fanciful fronds. They are the source of edible fiddleheads and make great costumes, magic wands, and tiny teepees.

Projects

+ Cutting Gardens
+ Dried Flowers
+ Native Plant Gardens
+ Shady Hideaway Gardens
+ Whimsy Gardens

Plant care

Ferns are incredibly easy to grow and disease and pest resistant, once planted in good, rich soil in a shady spot. Add compost when planting and keep them moist.

Grasses and Ornamental Grasses

Like ferns, there are hundreds of grasses, many of which are wonderful play toys for children. But beware—some varieties can have razor-sharp edges on their leaves and may not be suitable. However, the vast array of sizes, colors, and plumes make grasses well worth adding to a child's garden, especially to create a mysterious, hidden feel. Here are a few of my favorites:

- Japanese sweet flag (*Acorus gramineus*)—This grass is a glossy, solid green color; forms low, mounding clumps; and prefers moist soil.
- Variegated maiden grass (*Miscanthus sinensis* 'Morning Light')—This variety features 3-foot by 3-foot clumps of white-banded foliage and coppery-pink plumes in late summer.
- Dwarf fountain grass (*Pennisetum alopecuroides* 'Hameln')—This variety boasts 1- to 2-foot by 2- to 3-foot clumps of arching, narrow, green foliage topped with fuzzy, creamy catkins.

Plant care

With the wide variety of grasses and their unique needs and tolerances, you are best served finding a grass variety you like and reading about its specific care.

Projects

+ Container Gardens
+ Five-Senses Container Gardens
+ Holiday Projects: Fall Events
+ Native Plant Gardens
+ Science Experiment Gardens— Propagation
+ Seashore Gardens
+ Shady Hideaway Gardens

Hen and Chicks

(Sempervivum tectorum)

Please permit me a moment of nostalgia. Hen and chicks were the first plant I ever planted myself in my very own garden patch. I was seven or eight years old, and each time a new "chick," or pup, would appear, I would dig up the clump, carefully pull off the chick and plant it a few feet away to start its own colony. It's a wonder they all did not die (although the name *Sempervivum* does mean "live forever"). By the time we moved, the entire slope was covered. I have been too afraid to return to see if my hen and chicks have taken over a small town in Connecticut, but I would not be surprised. Hen and chicks are hardy, multipetaled succulents and come in a surprising array of variegated and green foliage with lovely, delicate flowers. I still love these plants and smile whenever I see them.

Projects

+ Houseplant
+ Five-Senses Container Gardens
+ Rock Gardens
+ Seashore Gardens
+ Whimsy Gardens

Plant care

Buy a nice, healthy plant with as many pups forming as possible. Plant it into well-drained soil with full sun. Once established, these plants are nearly indestructible.

79

Hosta

(*Hosta* spp.)

Hostas come in almost every shape, size, and variegation imaginable. Their shades range from clear yellow to almost deep blue, and their leaves can vary from pointed and tiny to huge and round. The leaves of these inspiring plants make fantastic fortresses, fans, and costumes. Hostas have flower spikes of blue, lavender, or white, which stand up above the foliage. They grow well near water and in deep shade, where some of the best playing takes place. Hostas are a must have for any children's garden!

Plant care

Hostas need at least partial shade; rich, well-drained soil; and plenty of water. They come in containers or as very small plants by mail. There are many to choose from, so take your time choosing. Make the rounds of garden centers or research online, and find the varieties that you like best. There will still probably be more than you have room for!

Projects

+ Cutting Gardens
+ Seashore Gardens
+ Shady Hideaway Gardens
+ Whimsy Gardens

Lamb's Ear

(Stachys byzantina)

No child's garden is complete without the soft, furry, silver-gray foliage of lamb's ear, which has delighted children for ages. In colonial times, mothers would use the leaves as pacifiers for their babies while in church. The soft, pink-and-lavender flower spikes can be enjoyed or cutback to keep the plant dense.

Projects

+ Five-Senses
  Container Gardens
+ Rock Gardens
+ Seashore Gardens
+ Whimsy Gardens

Plant care

Lamb's ear prefers full to partial sun and well-drained soil. To contain its floppy habit, shear the plant back in late summer. Good air circulation is necessary. This plant tolerates drought but not wet feet.

81

Lavender

(Lavandula angustifolia)

Who can resist lavender's delicate spikes of fragrant, blue-purple flowers and aromatic leaves? Lavender has soft, evergreen-like leaves on stems topped with spires of heavenly scented flowers. Children love to make bouquets and fairy wands with them, while adults love them to include them in sachets. Lavender makes a happy garden!

Plant care

Purchase well-rooted plants in late spring or summer. Full sun and well-drained soil are lavender's minimum requirements. They hate both the wet and the cold. Wet roots in winter are one sure way to lose them. Plant them into sandy soil in full sun. Once established, lavender is very drought tolerant.

Projects

+ Cutting Gardens
+ Dried Flowers
+ Five-Senses Container Gardens
+ Rock Gardens
+ Seashore Gardens

© Ellen Zachos

Lilyturf

(*Liriope* spp.)

Lilyturf is a wonderful plant for children to play with. It has evergreen foliage in a dense, rich green mat and tiny spikes of purple or white flowers in summer, followed by tiny, clinging, black-colored berries. As children, my friends and I used to carry the berry-crusted spikes around, conferring fairy-sized wishes on all who asked, until all of the berries had fallen off. Perhaps that's why there were always new patches of lilyturf throughout my neighborhood. There are some nice variegated forms, but I still prefer the solid green.

Projects

+ Five-Senses Container Gardens
+ Seashore Gardens
+ Shady Hideaway Gardens

Plant care

This lovely groundcover requires well-drained soil and tolerates sun or shade, but prefers some protection from the hot sun. It also divides easily and like organics at planting.

83

Primrose

(*Primula* spp.)

This scrumptious perennial is a true sign of warm weather. Primroses come in a rainbow of colors and forms ranging from dwarves to spikes. Primroses have cheerful faces and rich, green foliage. They also make excellent houseplants and are usually found in garden centers in midwinter, just when we need them the most.

Plant care

Primroses prefer light shade and rich, moist, humusy soil. They do not tolerate drought and require lots of organics when planting as well as mulching well before winter in colder areas.

Projects

+ Houseplant
+ Container Gardens
+ Native Plant Gardens
+ Rock Gardens

Purple Coneflower

(Echinacea purpurea)

Coneflowers are bright, daisy-headed flowers and are available in a growing array of colors and shapes. They are great for corsages and wild flower arrangements. Once seen only as large plants with purple flowers, they now come in forms ranging from dwarves to pompoms. Children love the bristly, button centers, and so do butterflies!

Projects

+ Butterfly Gardens
+ Cutting Gardens
+ Dried Flowers
+ Native Plant Gardens

Plant care

Purchase purple coneflowers as named varieties for specific traits, or ask a friendly gardener to give you some when they divide theirs. The plants thrive in sunny and windy sites. Remove faded flowers to stimulate new ones.

85

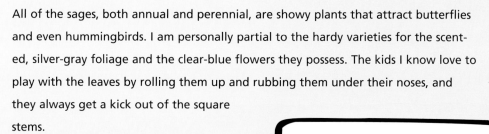

Sage and Hardy Sage

(*Salvia* spp.)

All of the sages, both annual and perennial, are showy plants that attract butterflies and even hummingbirds. I am personally partial to the hardy varieties for the scented, silver-gray foliage and the clear-blue flowers they possess. The kids I know love to play with the leaves by rolling them up and rubbing them under their noses, and they always get a kick out of the square stems.

Plant care

Pick a sage variety for the traits you like, and then plant these drought-tolerant annuals and perennials in warm, sunny spots with well-drained soil.

Projects

+ Container Gardens
+ Butterfly Gardens
+ Edible Gardens
+ Five-Senses Container Gardens

© Ellen Zachos

Stonecrop

(Sedum spp.)

Stonecrop is a large family of fleshy plants, all with fat, succulent leaves and star-like flowers. They come in an array of leaf and flower colors. Stonecrop can edge a bed, fall down a sloping rock garden, or stand sentry as fall foliage. Butterflies love them, and so do kids. There is a stonecrop for every sunny garden!

Projects

+ Butterfly Gardens
+ Five-Senses Container Gardens
+ Native Plant Gardens
+ Rock Gardens
+ Seashore Gardens

Plant care

There are so many wonderful stonecrops to choose from—pick one that suits your spot. They are all fun! Stonecrops prefer full sun and well-drained soil. They will even do well in poor soil. They can tolerate drought but not wet feet.

Rose Mallow

(Hibiscus moscheutos)

The huge, "dinner plate" flowers of swamp rose mallow never fail to delight. Bright white to pink to red petals, sometimes multicolored, and puffy stamens unfurl out of dramatic buds on huge, fleshy stalks. Though late to come out of the ground in the spring, they make up for it by flowering dramatically in August and September. Some varieties can grow to be 4 to 6 feet tall and are perfect for a child's hideaway or mini-forest.

Plant care

Choose varieties for specific traits, and then plant in rich, moist soil and full sun. Rose mallows make their first appearance very late in the spring, so don't assume they have died. They flower in August and early September.

Projects

+ Butterfly Gardens
+ Native Plant Gardens
+ Seashore Gardens
+ Whimsy Gardens

Bamboo can be a fort and
the makings of all kinds of tools.

Chapter 8

Planting for the Future: Silly Shrubs and Kid-Friendly Trees

I am a Tree Girl. I like most plants, but I love trees the very best. I didn't love nature first and then trees. I loved trees and from them learned to love the rest of nature. Please don't ever underestimate the value of a stroll in the woods together with your children. There are so many fascinating lessons to be learned from trees: the way roots travel in the soil; the way the wind strengthens trunks (like a weight machine!); why leaves have colors; and where the green goes when leaves change in the autumn. Trees are enthralling creatures and loyal, long-standing friends.

If you have a yard, be sure to include a few trees and shrubs specifically for your children to play with. Planting a tree can be a memorable family event. A tree can commemorate a loved one or an important milestone. I give trees as baby gifts. That way the tree grows with the child. A weeping mulberry or cherry can provide hours of shelter, companionship, and imaginative play. A serviceberry will teach kids about bird habitats and bring wildlife to your yard. Bamboo can be a fort and the makings of all kinds of tools. Plant the architecture of imagination in your yard, and watch what happens!

88

Bamboo

(Phyllostachys aurea)

Bamboo can be a blessing and also a curse. Kids love the tall, graceful stems and the many fun things they can do with them (for example, make fishing poles). But most of the varieties grown in the United States are very invasive. They are best planted in containers or kept well contained. However, if you have the right spot and are willing to do the work, a bamboo grove is a great haven for kids!

Projects

+ Shady Hideaway Gardens
+ Whimsy Gardens

Plant care

Depending on what zone you live in, there may be many or only a few kinds of bamboo that are suitable for your area. If running bamboo (one that sends runners underground, thus sending up new shoots) is your only option, be prepared to barrier it or plant it into containers; it can easily spread out of control. Bamboo can be planted into nearly any soil and will hold the ground even as it takes it over. Bamboo requires a good amount of water to get established, but afterwards it will withstand drought well. It can handle full sun to a fair amount of shade.

89

Blue Atlas Cedar

(*Cedrus atlantica* 'Glauca')

In a smaller garden, you will have to choose between a blue atlas cedar and a Norway spruce (see page 111); but in a perfect garden, you can have both. Upright blue Atlas cedars are tall, elegant, evergreen trees with silvery blue foliage that resembles an old man's craggy eyebrows. Another fun feature is the cones that stand straight up. They make wonderful climbing trees and good friends. The weeping variety makes a great hideaway or a personality-filled haven. Both forms grow quickly and with great character. This is one of my personal favorites.

Projects

+ Whimsy Gardens
+ Seashore Gardens

Plant care

Buy blue Atlas cedar as a young tree, and plant as a special event. It will grow quickly and become a cherished member of the family. Choose a sunny or partly sunny spot and well-drained, rich soil. Keep it watered when young, but never leave it in standing water.

90

Butterfly Bush

(Buddleia spp.)

These upright, arching shrubs with soft, silver-green foliage and deliciously fragrant flowers are beloved by humans and butterflies alike. They make a great, though short-lived, cut flower, but are best left on the shrub to draw butterflies to your garden. The plants make a great backbone for a butterfly garden or centerpiece for a wildflower border. Newer cultivars come in a variety of colors from white to purple and blue and red, and sizes ranging from dwarf to tall. The 'Nanho' dwarf series is excellent for smaller gardens.

Projects

+ Butterfly Gardens
+ Cutting Gardens
+ Native Plant Gardens
+ Seashore Gardens

Plant care

Choose a full-sun location, then pick a suitable cultivar for the amount of room you have available. One large plant or a trio of smaller shrubs makes a nice statement in your butterfly garden. Butterfly bushes prefer sandy, rich, well-drained soil.

Camellia

(Camellia spp.)

Tea is made from camellia leaves. If that fact is not cool enough, you have not seen a flower until you have seen the big, fat, gorgeous flowers on camellias. They come in a vast array of colors, as well as striped, ruffled, dotted, single, double, and multi-petaled varieties. When I helped make a float for the Rose Parade, camellia flower petals are what we used for the skin. And, never one to rest on its tea leaves, amazing new cultivars are introduced every year. Camellias used to be hardy only in the South, but now there are cultivars that can grow as far north as Boston. They make fantastic protected shrub borders.

Projects

+ Cutting Gardens
+ Whimsy Gardens

Plant care

Camellias prefer partial shade and good, rich, well-drained, acidic soil. They do well as an indoor plant, as long as they have a nice big container and good soil. Outside they require protection from extreme cold, sun, and winds, as much as possible.

Crape Myrtle

(*Lagerstroemia* spp.)

Crape myrtles are wonderful shrubs or small trees from the Deep South up to Zone 7. They have camouflage-patterned bark, graceful stems, panicles of beautiful white to pink to purple-red flowers in midsummer, gorgeous fall color, and then really cool seedpods that persist into winter. Kids love them for all of these things as well as their small tree stature, which makes children feel so at home.

Project

+ Whimsy Gardens

Plant care

Crape myrtles can be single- or multi-trunked trees. Choose a variety for the flower color and tree shape that you desire. These trees require lots of organics at planting and well-draining soil. They prefer full sun and protection from strong winds. They may die back in extreme cold.

93

Harry Lauder's Walking Stick

(Corylus avellana 'Contorta')

Harry Lauder was a vaudeville actor who had a twisted, contorted walking stick, probably made from this plant. This tree is a favorite of children, who like to twist among the limbs, play with the early spring catkins, and cut branches for their own purposes. It has a distinct personality in the garden and adds an element of fun, especially in the winter, when the branches are exposed.

Plant care

Harry Lauder's walking sticks can be found in most garden centers. Plant them with lots of organics and keep them well watered. They tolerate full sun to a fair amount of shade. They may occasionally get aphids, but a release of ladybugs will control the aphids. If the trees send straight suckers from the base, prune the suckers immediately or they will sap the strength from the grafted twisty trunks.

Project

+ Whimsy Gardens

94

Kousa Dogwood

(Cornus kousa)

Children love kousa dogwoods. I don't know if it is the mottled bark on the older limbs, the large, star-shaped flowers, the great fall color, or the fat, red berries that they find so appealing. Most likely all of the above, and who am I to argue? Kousa dogwood flowers one to two months after the American dogwood, once the plant has already leaved out, and is more disease resistant, so it's a winner all around!

Project

+ Whimsy Gardens

Plant care

Kousa dogwoods make a great family planting adventure. Purchase them as young saplings, plant them with love, and then watch them grow as your family does. They prefer sandy, rich, well-drained acidic soil and full to partial sun. They need to be watered deeply when young. Once established, they should handle all but the most severe droughts.

95

Lilac
(Syringa spp.)

Every child deserves to have a lilac shrub so that when they are grown up, the smell of lilacs can take them back to their childhood. The cones of the tiny, floret flowers are delicate and soft to the touch, yet they invade the senses and make everything feel new and fresh. Cultivars cover the gamut of white to deep purple, from dwarf to tree form, and from early to late spring bloomers. They make beautiful shrub borders.

Plant care

Lilacs prefer full sun and well-drained, alkaline (basic) soil. They need cold winters to stimulate flowering and do well at the seashore. Lilacs flower on old wood, so do not prune in the fall or early spring. Instead, prune just after the flowers fade. Cut out the oldest cane, straight to the base, every few years to inhibit borers and stimulate new shoots.

Projects

+ Cutting Gardens
+ Five-Senses Container Gardens
+ Seashore Gardens

Magnolia

(Magnolia spp.)

When I was a child in Connecticut, we had a giant southern magnolia in the backyard that was not supposed to be there. Botanists would come to visit and take cuttings and seeds. They would tell us that by all rights, the tree should not have survived even one of our winters, let alone the decades of winters that it already had. The flowers were huge, white, and incredibly fragrant. I felt a great attachment to that tree for taking the trouble to live there with us. I have loved magnolias ever since. There are many varieties, and you will love a handful of them once you get to know them; perhaps just as much as I still love southern magnolias, and sweetbay magnolias, and the incredibly silly bigleaf magnolias, and . . . you get the idea. The most popular varieties are saucer, southern, and star magnolias, but do a little research before you choose—there are so many varieties and new cultivars that are all worth a look.

Projects

+ Cutting Gardens
+ Whimsy Gardens

Plant care

Most magnolias prefer moist, rich soil, and partial sun. Some will tolerate wet roots, but most need good drainage. Protect them from cold winds, or you will lose early flower buds. Water trees through droughts, and fertilize lightly for the first few years until the tree is established.

© Pam Duthie

Norway Spruce

(Picea abies)

This tall, stately evergreen is not for a small yard. It is, however, possibly the best climbing tree ever, as well as being good for hiding under and playing in. The foliage is a rich, deep green, and the branches are wide and strong with drooping branchlets and scented cones.

The weeping variety (pictured) is much smaller (15 feet tall) and has a fortress-like structure. It is a great tree for playing hide-and-seek.

Plant care

This tree prefers well-drained soil that is rich in organic material. It will tolerate strong winds and fierce cold and does best in full sun.

Project

+ Whimsy Gardens

Pussy Willow
(Salix discolor)

and French Pussy Willow
(Salix caprea)

Pussy willow catkins are one of the joys of spring. Who cares that the plant is weedy and not very interesting the rest of the year? For a few, brief weeks, pussy willows rule. They are also easy to cut and force inside, and they root easily. They are one of the great sensory experiences of childhood, so if you can, make room for one in your garden.

Plant care

Find someone who is willing to give you a cutting and root it in water, or buy as a young plant. (There are many new, interesting cultivars, including pink and black varieties). Plant into enriched soil in a moist location (or plan on watering often). Pussy willows prefer full to partial sun and moist soil.

Projects

+ Cutting Gardens
+ Dried Flowers
+ Five-Senses Container Gardens
+ Native Plant Gardens
+ Seashore Gardens
+ Whimsy Gardens

99

Serviceberry, Juneberry, or Shadbush

(Amelanchier spp.)

This small, silver-barked tree can be single or multi-stemmed. It is relatively fast growing and has a lovely shape and form. It also has delicate, white flowers in the early spring, and then tiny, edible, blue-colored berries that beckon tiny fingers (and wildlife) to pick and eat them. The fall color is vibrant, and the whole effect of the tree in the garden is joyful. This delightful native tree is sure to make friends with small children.

Projects

+ Edible Gardens
+ Native Plant Gardens

Plant care

This native plant prefers a naturalistic setting—moist, well drained, slightly acidic soil, and partial shade. It will do well at the edge of a pond or in a woodland setting. It is wonderful planted where it can be seen from the house and just at the edge of wooded areas.

Weeping Cherry

(*Prunus subhirtella* 'Pendula')

Weeping cherry trees are beautiful additions to the home landscape. They are also a lot of fun. The "skirt" of a mature tree makes a great place for a tea party, a quiet spot for a good read, or the boundaries for a fort. The branches can be cut and forced in early spring; and when the tree is in flower, it is a delight to all of the senses. The falling petals are a powder of "snow" and make great mud pie toppings. It is an ornamental and has no fruit. Okay, maybe they are a little overused in the landscape, but can't you see why?

Projects

+ Cutting Gardens
+ Whimsy Gardens

Plant care

Let the kids pick this tree. Only they will know the perfect shape for their specific needs. Most weeping cherries are a "top graft," meaning that the weeping habit has been grafted onto an upright rootstock. Make sure you see the graft line and that it looks healthy. Plant your tree with lots of organic material mixed in. Water it deeply once a week for the first year. Ask the children to refrain from climbing on it for the first two years (or plant it when they are too small for climbing.) Weeping cherries need full sun and well-drained, rich soil.

Caution: The seeds, bark, and leaves of weeping cherry trees are poisonous.

© Raintree Nursery

101

Weeping Mulberry

(Morus alba 'Pendula')

A weeping mulberry was one of my first forts. It was also one of my best friends. I could wind myself into that tree and hang upside down while spying on everyone outside its leafy fringe. That tree and I had some good times. Our "non-fruiting" mulberry made enough deep purple berries to make jam and pies each year and also stain the kitchen linoleum permanently. You might like the fruit or prefer to pick one that really is non-fruiting.

Plant care

It may be hard to find these, as many people do not appreciate their ornamental value. Do some research and pick your tree by its shape. Weeping mulberries prefer full sun to light shade, tolerate a wide range of soils, including seashore conditions, and are drought tolerant once established. They will be happiest, especially the fruiting varieties, in moist, rich soil. Prune only if your tree is becoming unruly.

Projects

+ Seashore Gardens
+ Shady Hideaway Gardens
+ Whimsy Gardens

Allergic reactions vary from person to person, and children are especially sensitive.

A Few Plants to Never Use with Kids

There are two ways in which plants can harm people:

• Ingesting: Ingesting plants can hurt people in a number of ways. They can cause pain in the mouth or they can be poisonous—causing diarrhea, vomiting, closing of the air passages, neurological damage, or choking.

• Touching: Even just touching certain plants can cause dermatitis, rashes, or swelling.

It is important to remember, though, that children and animals can choke on the parts of any plant. Allergic reactions vary from person to person, and children are especially sensitive. Be alert when introducing children to any new environment. Immediately call the Poison Center at 1-800-222-1222 if anyone might have swallowed a possibly poisonous plant or is having a reaction to a plant. The following plants are ones that you should never let children near unsupervised.

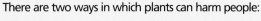

- **Azaleas:** This plant can cause serious illness or death if ingested.
- **Castor bean:** Can cause serious illness or death if ingested.
- **Daffodil:** Can cause diarrhea or vomiting if ingested; may cause contact dermatitis in some people.
- **Daphne:** Can cause serious illness or death if ingested.

- **Delphinium:** Can cause serious illness or death if ingested.
- **Foxglove:** Can cause serious illness or death if ingested.
- **Hydrangeas:** The flowers can cause serious illness or death if ingested; the plant may cause contact dermatitis in some people.
- **Lantana:** The berries can cause serious illness or death if ingested.
- **Laurel:** Can cause diarrhea or vomiting if ingested.
- **Lily of the valley:** Can cause serious illness or death if ingested.
- **May apple:** Can cause serious illness or death if ingested.
- **Mistletoe:** Can cause diarrhea or vomiting if ingested.
- **Mushrooms:** Do not eat any mushroom you cannot definitively identify. Many are toxic.
- **Oleander:** Can cause serious illness or death if ingested; the plant may cause contact dermatitis in some people.
- **Rhododendron:** Can cause serious illness or death if ingested.
- **Wisteria:** Can cause diarrhea or vomiting if ingested.

This is by no means a complete list, only a few plants children may be likely to come in contact with. If you are unsure of a plant's identification or if it is potentially hazardous to children (or pets), contact your county extension agent.

Chapter 10

Fun Projects and Garden Ideas

Gardening Basics

Plants are surprisingly forgiving. They want to grow. If we give them the bare minimum to get by, often they will do it, in spite of us. So what is the bare minimum?

Soil. Seeds or plants with healthy roots. Sun. Moisture, Hospitable growing conditions. And nutrients.

But here is the tricky part—all plants do not like the same things. I love mint chip ice cream and cannot stand pralines and cream. My best friend loves pralines and cream and thinks I am crazy to like mint chip. Plants are the same way. (No, as far as I know, they do not like mint chip, or any other kind of ice cream for that matter.) Ideal conditions for one plant might possibly kill another. If you are going to plant a garden, you must first observe your conditions, or the conditions you are able to create, and then pick plants that are best suited to those conditions.

And do not think that if you are unsuccessful once or twice that you have a "black thumb." You are not getting off that easily. There are endless resources available to you, especially Web sites. I have included a few in the resource section of this book. Another relationship that will serve you well is to find a reputable garden center or extension service in your area. Get to know someone there, then ask him or her any questions you have.

Soil

When planting trees, shrubs, and perennials, add rich, organic humus or composted manure. *But* determine what additives you need by the kind of soil you are starting with. If you have loose, crumbly soil that already drains well, you do not need to add sand. If the soil is heavy and holds together when you squeeze it, you *should not* add sand (clay plus sand equals concrete). Compost or composted manure (don't worry—it smells nice) are almost always good to add. Use clean, fresh potting mix if planting into containers. Never use garden soil, as it most likely has bacteria.

Ralph Snodsmith, who was a professor of mine, used to say, "When you are planting is the only time in the life of the plant you are able to get underneath it." Good to remember! Err on the side of lots of good additives rather than skimping.

Seeds and Young Plants

If you always buy the last plant on the picked-over table at the grocery store, throw it into a pot in the backyard, and then wonder why your plants always die, shame on you! Plants cannot be on death's doorstep when you buy them, and they need to be pampered through their childhood.

Most seeds arrive healthy, but if they clump together or look as if something is growing on them, throw them out and get new ones. Plant seeds into clean soil. Seedlings must be kept moist until they can fend on their own. When putting young plants into the soil or ground, gently tease their roots open so the roots grow out into the surrounding soil rather than staying snarled up. Always water immediately after planting to soak the roots and remove air pockets in the soil.

Sun

All plants need light, but not all plants need the same amount of light. This is a great thing considering that no two spots in most yards get exactly the same amount of sun. If you have a bright, sunny place, find the right plant for it (for exam-

Gooey Fun

Kids love to watch moisture crystals grow, and they love the slimy feel of them. Some adults think they are pretty cool, too.

When you are planting, put some moisture crystals aside for your own experiments. Place some in a clear cup or container and add

water. You can watch the crystals turn to gel. You can also add some food coloring to the water when you are making the gel and make different colored gel. *Be careful:* The crystals will expand as they turn to gel, so do not fill the cup too high or the gel will overflow.

Once the gel is formed, you can squish it between your fingers and have all kinds of fun. The gooey feeling may gross out some grownups—and probably some little sisters, too!

ple, butterfly bush, lilac, and sunflower). But if your yard isn't so sunny, there are wonderful plants for your conditions, too. Ferns, serviceberries, and blueberries will all take some shade. There are even plants that do best in full shade, such as under large trees. The most important thing is to discover how much light you really get, and then pick the plants that like those conditions.

Moisture

The same is true for water—all plants need some water. But some plants love it, and some want only a little. Whether you have a permanent swamp or a virtual desert, there are plants that will be happy in your yard. Do the research, pick plants you will love and that will love your yard, and plant them properly. Once they are in place, don't forget about them. Some plants may only need extra water the first year, while they get their roots established. Some may always need to be wet. Others may be fine except in severe drought. Watch your plants. Watch the leaves and the springiness of the stems. They will tell you how they're doing.

Containers are tricky until you get the hang of them. They *must* have drainage, or else the roots will rot. They also will dry out faster than the soil in the garden, so check planters for dryness every day until you get a sense of how often they need water. If you are planting water-loving plants, consider planting containers with SoilMoist or other water-retaining crystals. And make sure the drainage holes don't clog up mid-season.

Hospitable Growing Conditions

Sounds impressive, huh? What it means is how hot or cold, windy or calm, humid or dry it is, as compared with what your plants want. Tulips hate hot summers, but rose moss loves them. Lilacs need cold winters, which can harm crape myrtles. Ferns like humidity, which will promote powdery mildew on lilacs. It is not a question of

good or bad. It is a question of knowing what you have and what your plants need.

Nutrients

Just as humans need vitamins to stay healthy and strong, plants need to get their nutrients, too. Usually they can get what they need from the soil. But if the soil is depleted, or if the plants are in containers where they cannot reach what they need, or if they are especially nutrient-hungry plants (i.e., most annuals), it is a good idea to feed them. Annuals do best with water-soluble fertilizers, which are immediately accessible. But follow the directions—too much fertilizer can kill your plants! Trees and shrubs do best with timed-release fertilizers, which give food steadily to the roots over the growing season and do not "burn" the roots.

One more thing to take into consideration is the acidity (pH) of the soil. This will not be a big concern with annuals, but for trees, shrubs, and perennials, knowing the acidity of your soil and the acid preferences of your plants might be the difference between a truly happy plant and one that limps along. Your new best friend at the extension service or garden center will be able to test your soil for you and tell you if your plant choices are good matches.

I know this all sounds a little overwhelming, but it doesn't have to be. Jump in, have fun, be observant, and ask questions when things look wrong—you know, act like a kid! The process of planting is actually a great way to teach kids so many concepts about science, chemistry, and life in general. Kids are incredibly observant and seem to instinctively understand what plants need. Take your child to visit your plants, observe them, and talk about whether they look happy and what might be the reasons they are or aren't. Then do the research either online or at the extension service or garden center. You'll be teaching your kids skills and concepts that will help them later in life. You will have fun, and you just might learn something too!

Bulb Container Gardens

Most bulbs (and corms, too) need to be chilled before they will flower. It is one of Mother Nature's little tricks. But chilling bulbs is really not that hard to do, and it is so much fun to watch them bloom in the house in winter.

Good Bulb Choices

Crocus
Grape hyacinth
Snowdrop
Tulip

Placing bulbs in a pot and then adding soil to cover them is much easier than digging holes and planting bulbs in a full pot.

Basic Requirements

- A few small, shallow pots that will fit two or three bulbs per pot (Bulb pans are best, of course.)
- A few bulbs (or corms) for each pot you will be planting
- Potting soil
- One or two glasses that can hold one single bulb

Steps for Forcing Bulbs

Bulbs that flower in the springtime can only be found to buy in the fall. That is because they need to go into the ground to get a cold nap. Then when the soil around them warms, they wake up and begin to flower. We can force bulbs by giving them a cold nap and waking them up early.

There are two ways to force bulbs. One is to plant them into a pot in the fall and bury the pot outside, bringing the pot in after six to ten weeks. This works in USDA Hardiness Zone 7 or colder, where winter temperatures go down below 40° F. The other is to put bulbs in the refrigerator for six to ten weeks, then plant them. Both methods work, but the refrigerator method has more risks. Bulbs can rot in the fridge, and they must be kept away from ripening fruit, which releases a gas that can kill them.

Bulbs must be kept dry, have good air circulation, and be kept separate from any food. They do best alone in the crisper wrapped in paper towels. But for some reason, some of us aren't always willing to give up a crisper for ten weeks. Go figure! And no, they cannot go into the freezer. They turn to mush!

1 To plant into pots, fill pots to 3 to 4 inches beneath the rim with soil. Set a few bulbs into the soil, far enough apart that they are not touching. Make sure they are right side up! Fill the pots with soil to just above the tops of the bulbs. Press down gently.

2 Give the pots a nice soak to settle the roots in and fill in any air holes in the soil. Make sure the pots drain well or the roots will rot.

3 Now put the pots outside. Either dig a hole and set the pots into the ground just up to the rim, or find a natural depression and bury the pots with leaves. And then leave them.

4 Six to ten weeks later, depending on how cold the weather is, dig up one pot and

bring it inside to a place that is 50 to 70° F and out of full sun. Water it once gently.

5 Within a week or two, you should see little green shoots growing. You will get to watch the leaves and stems shoot up and flower. Keep it watered as needed (whenever the soil dries out), but do not let it sit in wet soil. Bulbs can rot very easily.

6 Once you see sprouts on your first pot, bring in another. Then bring in a pot or two every week or two until you run out. You could have flowers all the way into spring!

When the plants have finished flowering, keep the pot in a sunny spot inside until the foliage dies back, then cut it back. In the spring you can plant them out in the garden, although they won't flower until the next year, if at all. Or you can pitch them out and start again next year.

Hanging Baskets and Container Gardens

If you are not planting right into the ground, you will be planting into some kind of container. And it really *is* easy, as long as you understand what you are doing. But if you don't know or don't think it through, planting into a container can be a disaster.

Quite a few of the projects in this chapter will be planted in containers, so these basics are important to know. You can apply them to just about every container garden you plant, whether for kids or adults.

Plants

The types of plants you can use are entirely up to you. If you want a container of all red, yellow, blue, white, or orange flowers, go for it! If you want to mix all kinds of plants together, you can. Some plants will grow tall, others will stay small, and others can flow down the sides of your pot or basket. Or you can plant veggies, herbs, or strawberries—

your container garden can then be a snack bowl.

Just be sure that all of the plants in the same container all need the same thing. A mix of plants that need full sun and shade will not turn out well no matter where you plant it. If you put plants that need very little water and plants that need a lot of water together, one of those types will be happy and the other will die.

Planting

When you plant in containers, never use soil from the garden. There are diseases and bugs in garden dirt that can cause your plants to get sick, wilt, or even die. Your plants' roots need to be taken care of so your container garden will be healthy. Make sure you use good potting soil or compost mix suitable for your plantings.

Container plants may also have problems with their roots. As the roots grow, they will reach the edges or bottom of the pot, hit a wall, and turn. If they do that enough, they will become a great big knot, like a snarl in your hair. Then, because the roots will be competing with each other for water and nutrients, the whole mass will die, often suddenly. So leave lots of room between plants when planting a container, to give them room to grow. Always plan on spacing plants twice as wide as the root area is.

When placing the plants, loosen up their roots so there are no stranglers, and lay them out into the container. Put enough soil in the container that you can lay the spread-out roots on top and fill in around the plants with soil, just to the place where their roots and stems meet (the "crown" of the plant). The potting soil should come up to an inch or so below the rim of the pot so that when you water, the water will sink in and not spill over the top and potentially hurt the plants or get your container all muddy.

Water

Containers prevent your plants from getting the water and food they need from the soil in your garden. Plants in containers also feel the heat or cold

Butterflies will come to eat and stay to lay eggs.

© Jill Dessauer

more than garden plants will and usually dry out more quickly. So you will need to water them more often and give them fertilizer. You can add moisture crystals to the potting mix to help keep the soil wet. Moisture crystals, such as SoilMoist, absorb water and turn into a gel and will release water slowly as the soil around the plants dries out. You will want to add these crystals if your plants need a lot of water, the area will bake in the sun, or you often forget to water.

At the same time, good drainage is important. Plants can die from soggy soil, lack of good drainage, or humid, poor air circulation. Drainage holes, good porous material at the bottom of the planter (such as pebbles or small rocks), and moisture crystals will aid your plant success greatly.

Butterfly Gardens

Once we become aware of all the amazing creatures with whom we share this world, it becomes rewarding to see them up close and personal. One way to do this is to plant the things they like so they will live near us. Here are some plants and other ideas for attracting butterflies to your yard.

Basic Requirements
- Butterfly-attracting plants
- A shallow pan of water with rocks in it for butterflies to perch on. A butterfly unreels his proboscis (which looks like a trunk) into the water, most likely to suck up minerals from the rocks. This is called "puddling." Butterflies are especially likely to do this where there is salty material in the water.
- Full sun! Butterflies are solar powered.
- A dark-colored rock for them to perch on while they "recharge." You are especially likely to see this behavior first thing in the morning after a cool night. They will slowly fold and unfold their wings, turning to get the best sun on their bodies.

Good Plant Choices

ANNUALS

Brazilian verbena	Parsley
Carrots	(for caterpillars)
(for caterpillars)	Passionflower
Cosmos	Spider flower
Dill (for caterpillars)	Verbena
Forget-me-not	Zinnia
Hollyhock	
(for caterpillars)	

PERENNIALS

Bee balm	Sage
Daylily	Stonecrop
Purple coneflower	Swamp rose mallow

SHRUB

Butterfly bush

Simple Butterfly Garden Ideas

Butterfly-attracting annuals can be planted into large planters or containers so they can be changed each year. Be sure the pots have good drainage and are in full sun. (See the container-planting section on page 123.)

Flowering annuals can also be put into hanging baskets and hung where they can be seen from the house or in a spot where a ground planting is not practical.

Butterflies will not remain very long in a place where they cannot lay eggs. Their lives as butterflies can be as short as two weeks, and they do not have time to waste. Be sure to plant parsley, dill, and hollyhocks near butterfly-attracting flowers. They will come to eat and stay to lay eggs. Then in a few weeks, you will begin to find cute caterpillars consuming your herbs. *Do not kill them!* These are the next generation of butterflies growing in your yard.

Cutting Gardens

There is nothing more fun than going into your own cutting garden and getting armfuls of fresh cut flowers for your home or to give to a friend. A cutting garden is simply an area planted with flowers that make good cut flowers. You can plant them in rows or make a wide bed that is pretty to look at. But whatever you do, plant flowers that will bloom all season long and fill bouquets and vases for months.

It's best to cut flowers first thing in the morning before the heat of the sun wilts them. Use very sharp scissors or garden shears (an adult should do

Arranging flowers in a vase can be fun, but not as much fun as sticking them in a watermelon!

this), and make a clean, slightly diagonal cut through the stem. Then sink them directly into very warm water.

Good Plant Choices

ANNUALS

Brazilian verbena	Marigold
Canterbury bells	Money plant
Cockscomb	Pansy
Coleus (foliage)	Snapdragon
Cosmos	Spider flower
Dahlia	Statice
Daylily	Sunflower
Dill (flower)	Sweet pea
Forget-me-not	Viola
Globe amaranth	Zinnia

BULBS

Crocus	Tulip

PERENNIALS

Balloon flower	Mint
Bee balm	(flowers and foliage)
Black-eyed Susan	Purple coneflower
Ferns (foliage)	Thyme
Hosta (foliage)	
Lavender	

TREES AND SHRUBS

Butterfly bush	Magnolia
Camellia	Pussy willow
Lilac	Weeping cherry

Basic Requirements

- Full sun
- Good, enriched soil
- A steady water supply
     (soaker hoses or irrigation)
- Stakes for the taller, floppy plants

Cut Flower Garden Ideas

- If you do not have a lot of garden space, a small grouping of plants can be planted into containers and cut from there.
- If you have room, the cutting garden can be located near the kitchen or hidden from view. Your other gardens can be kept in more visible places around your house.
- You want the beds or containers to be orderly enough that you can cut what you need without hurting the surrounding plants.
- Though annuals will be the first choice, perennials and shrubs, such as butterfly bush and lilac, are wonderful additions in arrangements as well.
- Be sure to include foliage in your cut arrangements, especially coleus, fern, and mint, for their color, texture and scent.
- There is no "right" or "wrong" flower arrangement. Anything a child puts together and is happy with is right!

Dried Flower Gardens

A cut flower arrangement is lovely. A dried flower arrangement is lasting art! Growing, cutting, and then keeping the beauty produced can be fulfilling for children and adults alike.

Basic Requirements

- Flowers that dry well
- A cool, dark, open, well-ventilated place to let them dry
- Twine or wire for the stems
- Tissue paper for pressing flowers
- A few heavy books for pressing

Steps for Drying Flowers

1. As with cut flowers, it is best to cut the flowers first thing in the morning before the heat of the sun wilts them. Use very sharp scissors or garden shears (an adult should do this), and make a clean, slightly diagonal cut through the stem. Try to include as much stem as possible because flowers with long stems are easier to arrange.
2. Remove the foliage from the stems up to just below the flower heads.

Good Plant Choices

ANNUALS

Cockscomb	Strawflower
Globe amaranth	Sunflower
Money plant	
Statice	

PERENNIALS

Ferns	Purple coneflower
Lavender	

SHRUB

Pussy willow

3. Wrap some twine or wire around the ends of the stems, singly or in small bunches, so the flowers do not crowd each other and bend unnecessarily.
4. Hang the flowers upside down in a cool spot, away from direct sunlight, with good air circulation and plenty of room for air between bunches.

5. Check them every few days. They should begin to dry out and get papery. They should not mold, begin to smell funny, or start to grow things. If they do, you should throw them out.
6. When the flowers feel dry to the touch, leave them another week. Then take them down, unwrap them, and carefully sort through them. Remove any unnecessary leaves.
7. Create arrangements with flowers, foliage, ribbons, and whatever else your imagination inspires!

Edible Gardens

A long time ago, way back before televisions had remote controls, people grew most if not all of their own food. Today, most kids assume that food comes from the grocery store and that plants are there to look pretty. I love to tend vegetable gardens with kids, but even more, I love to plant things we can just nip off and nibble—fruits, vegetables, and even flowers! And there are plenty. Here are some fun "non-vegetable" ideas. Vegetable gardens are talked about later in the book. *Caution:* Do not use chemicals on your edibles!

Basic Requirements
Each of the edible plants below has different needs. Some are annuals, some perennials, some shrubs, and one tree. You will need to give some thought to what space you have available and if this is the best choice for the spot. But there are few feelings better than nibbling fresh nasturtium leaves or plucking tender daylily flowers, and then battering and frying them with your children. Or using geraniums as herbs as well as to make tea. Or being able to make a pie from fruit you picked in your own yard—priceless!

Simple Edible Garden Ideas
- Plant nasturtiums outside the kitchen on a trellis, then pick some leaves and flowers to toss into fresh salads.

Good Plant Choices

ANNUALS

Dandelion	Sunflower
Geranium	Viola
Nasturtium	Watermelon
Pansy	

PERENNIALS

Daylily	Sage
Mint	Strawberry

TREES AND SHRUBS

Apple	Raspberry
Blueberry	Serviceberry

- Pansies will flower in fall and again in the spring. If the summer is hot they will die, but in cool, shady spots they can be cut back to flower again in the fall. The flowers look great in ice cubes or on salads.
- Plant sunflowers where they will get plenty of sun and water and where they will not block the light other plants need. As the seed heads ripen, you will have to fight the birds for them, but it is well worth the effort! (I plant twice as much as I want and let the birds have some, too.)
- Strawberries can be planted onto mounds or terraced pyramids. This way the plants, natu-

rally a groundcover, can be found and get more sunlight, so you get bigger strawberries.

- Blueberries and raspberries are tough shrubs. Blueberries can be planted in the shade and in very moist spots. Raspberries prefer a little more sun and will spread rapidly. Raspberry bushes have thorns, but the little raspberries are well worth the risk. However, gardening gloves and long sleeves are highly recommended when harvesting raspberries.

- Planting a tree is a major step but an apple is a fine tree to plant. Some people like to plant trees to commemorate special events or people. Or you may want to start your own orchard. Whatever the reason, apples need very rich, organic soil and full sun. Depending on the variety, you may need to plant two for good cross-pollination. There are also some nice dwarf varieties available. Do some research, and then enjoy watching your tree grow! Beware, however, all parts of the apple tree except the fruit itself (including the seeds) can make you sick if you eat enough of them! Stick to the healthy, yummy apples, and leave the leaves and seeds alone.

A pie is truly homemade when you fill it with berries you grew.

Fun Fact

Apples are an important part of American history and were one of the most important crops for early Americans. Apples can be eaten raw, baked, broiled, sautéed, pureed, boiled into apple butter, and pressed for cider. Cider vinegar can be used to preserve foods, which was very important in the days before refrigeration.

Five-Senses Container Gardens

Too often adults ignore everyday things. But children have not lost their sense of wonder. Here are some plants that kids will enjoy for their different sensations. Choose a plant for each of the senses—sight, smell, sound, taste, and touch. These stimulating plants may even make grownups pay attention. Sometimes the best antidote to a high-tech world is a high-touch garden!

Basic Requirements
- Potting mix (not garden dirt)
- Large container with good drainage
- Place plants with similar needs together

Simple Five-Senses Garden Ideas
- A five-senses container planting is a great way to get kids involved in using their senses. Let kids plant up a container and watch it grow. Talk with them about how the different plants look, feel, smell, taste (pictured), and sound. Go outside to listen to the rainfall on the plants. Then let them water the plants and compare the sounds. You will be amazed at what kids notice when you let them.
- Generally, lilacs prefer to be in the ground. But if you use a dwarf variety, such as 'Miss Kim' or 'Palibin', and put it in a very large container, you can be successful.
- This sensory container garden is especially fun with less mobile children or children with special needs, who may not often get to be responsible for many things and who will revel in the sensory stimulation.
- You can also extend your container garden into an entire senses-themed garden. Pick out flowers, herbs, shrubs, and grasses at the garden center based on how they smell, feel, taste, and sound. Then lay back or sit down in your garden and enjoy a total-sensory experience!

Good Plant Choices

Basil (yummy)

Cockscomb (funky on the fingers)

Coleus (great colorful leaves)

Lamb's ear
  (as soft and furry as, well, a lamb's ear)

Hen and chicks
  (great to touch and fun to watch)

Ice plant
  (edible, fragrant, and great to touch)

Lavender (delicious to smell)

Lilac (possibly the best smell ever)

Lilyturf
  (Make some noise—hold a blade between your thumbs and use it as a reed.)

Mint (delicious)

Nasturtium
  (fun to pinch off and nibble—spicy)

Ornamental grasses (soothing sounds)

Parsley (easy and yummy)

Pussy willow (wonderfully soft)

Sage (great smell)

Stonecrop
  (really fun, succulent leaves and soft, furry flowers)

Thyme
  (walk on it for the smell, pick it for the taste)

Holiday Projects

Kids love gardening projects but never more so than when they have a purpose. Here are a few simple useful projects for specific events. These are just a few of the projects I have done with kids. What ones can you add?

St. Patrick's Day

Plant clover seed into moist soil inside an upside-down plastic party hat (preferably green!) just after President's Day. By St. Patrick's Day, you should have a lovely crop of (if you're lucky!) four-leaf clovers with which to celebrate.

Spring Holidays

Pansy plants or already-forced bulbs from the store can be carefully planted into decorated cups or pots and given as Easter, Passover, or the first day of spring presents.

There's nothing a mom seems to like more than a hand-planted plant, especially when it's planted into something silly, like a shoe or a baseball cap or a pail. Plant a container of annuals for Mom's Day, so she knows she's loved all summer long!

I used to give my dad gift certificates for a day of work in the garden for Father's Day. We had some fun times together. If that isn't your idea of fun, make him a piece of garden art out of twigs and stones. Or buy him a blueberry bush, something you'll both enjoy for years!

Summer Events

A small pot of annuals, or even a single plant such as a geranium, makes a lovely end-of-the-school-year present for teachers or school staff. You can jazz up the pots with paint or by gluing on school-related decorations.

Planting up a big pot of annuals, or even a whiskey barrel full, can be a great family Memorial Day project to enjoy all summer long.

Plant a container or a garden bed "red, white, and blue" if you are planning ahead for

Mom will think of you every time she looks at these flowers.

Independence Day. But remember: Plan ahead. By July there are not many annuals for sale in the stores.

If you have been growing berries, you can make an Independence Day pie. You can also decorate a cake to look like an American flag with blueberries and strawberries. You can find great Fourth of July recipes in cookbooks or on the Internet.

Fall Events

If you want sunflowers in October, plant their seeds on the Fourth of July.

Pots of pansies and violas make wonderful Grandparents' Day presents.

Late August through Labor Day is the time to plant a big bowl of lettuce seed, if you want autumn salads. They thrive in the cool weather. It is also a great back-to-school project.

Hairy Harry is a classic classroom project (pictured right). Decorate a pot or paper cup with ears and a face. Fill it with soil and just dampen it. (Drainage holes are a good idea, but do not make them too big.) Spread a thin layer of some type of grass seed, such as Kentucky bluegrass, across the top, and then put the pot in a sunny window. Once the grass grows two or three inches tall, you can start cutting it, giving Hairy Harry "haircuts" as needed. This is a great first present home to the parents (as long as you also send care instructions) or a rainy-day project at home.

Thanksgiving

Dried flowers are a wonderful three-step project for the Thanksgiving table. Plant the flowers in the spring. Harvest and hang them anytime from late August until late September, depending on the plant. Make arrangements or glue the flowers onto cut out forms in the weeks just before Thanksgiving to use as the homemade family dinner centerpiece. But be sure to keep them away from open flames! (Find instructions for drying flowers on page 127.)

Christmas and Hanukkah

Evergreen magnolia leaves glued onto rings make wonderful holiday wreaths. If you don't have a magnolia tree handy, you can often buy the leaves at the florist.

- Pre-chilled crocus, planted in November, can make a lovely blue and white holiday centerpiece for the Hanukkah table.
- Species tulips, either prechilled or bought and chilled by the first week of September, can be planted for a really extraordinary Christmas centerpiece. I like to put them in a rustic wooden box, then tie the box with a plaid ribbon.
- Flowers that were pressed at the end of the summer can come out in time for the holidays and make wonderful cards when glued to cardboard stock.

After putting a face on a cup or pot, kids can fill the "head" with potting mix, sprinkle grass seed, and water. Soon they will have a full head of "hair" to trim and style.

Native Plant Gardens

We are becoming a global garden very quickly. Yet it is nice to know what plants were here before we started using plants from all around the world. The following plants are all North American natives. Many people believe that native plants are better suited to the environment and that they are better choices to plant since local wildlife depend on them. Natives make a nice starting point for discussions on ecosystems as well as the symbiotic relationship between plants and animals. There are also just some really great native plants that are fun to grow and nice to have around!

Basic Requirements

None of these plants have the same requirements. North America is a big place, and our plants have adapted to their own individual niches. One of the nice things to learn from these plants is how different they are and how each is well suited to its environment.

Simple Native Plant Garden Ideas

A plains garden will have very different plants than a woodlands garden or a tropical garden. Planting your garden naturally leads to discussions of how different native plants adapted to their surroundings and why certain plants do better in your garden than others. Use your garden to inspire conversation, debate, and further research with children. You can plan a garden project with one plant from each state, a small grouping of plants for each microenvironment in your area, or plants from each region of the country. Do some research at the library, on the Internet, or your local garden to help you choose plants for your Native Plant theme.

There are many, many other native North American plants besides these, but these are ones I have had success with. Try some from your state or region, and have fun!

Good Plant Choices

ANNUALS

Carrot	Pansy
Cockscomb	Passionflower
Corn	Spider flower
Gazania	Sunflower
Globe amaranth	Sweet pea
Green bean	Verbena
Impatiens	Viola
Lettuce	Zinnia

PERENNIALS

Black-eyed Susan	Ornamental grasses
Ferns (many varieties)	Primrose
Grasses (many varieties)	Purple coneflower
	Stonecrop
Kentucky bluegrass	Strawberry
Mint	Swamp rose mallow

TREES AND SHRUBS

Apple	Pussy willow
Blueberry	Raspberry
Butterfly bush	Serviceberry

POND OR SWAMP PLANTS

Lotus	Water lily
Venus flytrap	

Plant a Rainbow

A rainbow is made up of all of the colors in the spectrum—even some we humans cannot see. The ones we can see show up in this order: red, orange, yellow, green, blue, indigo, and violet. (Many lists of a rainbow's colors do not include indigo because it is hard for humans to see the different shades of blue. You may choose to plant your rainbow garden with only six colors, going from blue to violet and skipping indigo.) While planting a rainbow garden with your children—whether you use just one plant of each color or a whole arc—you can teach them about colors, the spectrum of light (with a glass prism, if you have one), sunlight, rain, the way the earth moves, physics, René Descartes (the first person to figure out the physics of how and why rainbows appear), and different cultures' stories about rainbows! What's more, a rainbow garden is beautiful all summer long.

Basic Requirements

This annual garden will do best in full sun, but the specifics will depend on the plants you choose. Organic, well-drained soil is probably best. When you buy your plants, pick them for color and similar size, if possible. If not possible, try for taller red-flowered plants in the back leading to small violet-flowered in front. For example, you could plant nearly red/brown sunflowers in back and pretty violet petunias in front.

Good Plant Choices

Canterbury bells
Cockscomb
Cosmos
Dahlia
Forget-me-not
Fuchsia
Gazania
Geranium
Globe amaranth
Hollyhock
Impatiens
Marigold
New Guinea impatiens
Petunia
Rose moss
Snapdragon
Statice
Strawflower
Sunflower
Tuberous begonia
Verbena
Zinnia

Some Simple Rainbow Garden Ideas

- Many plants come in so many different flower colors, you can create your whole rainbow garden with only one or two plant types, or you can use a different plant for each color of the rainbow.
- Pick a spot in the garden where you can plant a row of each color, slightly arched, for the full rainbow effect.
- Have your rainbow garden grow back year after year by substituting colorful perennials for annuals.
- For fun and variety, plant a window box with one of each color.

Rock Gardens

A rock garden is a great way to make a hard-to-plant area look nicer. It is also a great way to take a "normal" part of the garden and make it stand out. A rock garden is defined as a rock outcropping, planted with low-growing plants from the mountainous regions of the world. It can be an existing rock pile, built up rocks like a cliff, or low rocks with plants in between. Whichever style you prefer, the soil should be loose and sandy, and the plants should be tough and low growing.

Basic Requirements
- Attractive stones or rocks
- Preferably a slope or banked area
- Rich, sandy soil
- Full to mostly full sun

Simple Rock Garden Ideas

My first garden ever was an impossible slope with killer rocks in Connecticut. I somehow got and planted one hen and chicks plant, then I pulled off the pups and replanted them as fast as they grew. By the time I moved, just a few years later, the hillside was covered and the pups were having pups.

Create a natural-looking rock cropping with extra or unwanted rocks from the yard. A hillside or a flat surface works well. Fill the spaces in between the rocks with soil mixed well with sand and compost. Tuck plants into the nooks and crannies between the rocks. Water the plantings well to get them established, and then only as needed after.

An alternative is to take a stone planter, such as the one pictured on the opposite page, and plant it up with succulents and other rock garden plants. That guarantees a rock garden wherever you feel the urge to have one!

Good Plant Choices

ANNUALS

Ice plant	Rose moss
(in warm climates)	Sweet William
Pansy	Viola

BULBS

Crocus
Grape hyacinth
Tulip

PERENNIALS

Balloon flower	Primrose
Hen and chicks	Stonecrop
Lamb's ear	Thyme
Lavender	

Science Experiments

There is a school of learning that says there is no educational curriculum that cannot be taught through the garden. I love that! It has been my experience, especially when playing with children, that complex thoughts like the alphabet, multiplication, genetics, gravity, and the spectrum of light (as well as God, life and death, and life's greater meaning) just seem to make more sense when we are outside in nature.

With that in mind, why not stack the deck a little? Try planting and planning activities that lead to educational discussions. These do not have to be serious classroom discussions. These can be conversations to have with your children as you take nature walks or as you plant together. Your wondering allows your children to wonder too, which inspires a sense of awe and curiosity. Once awakened, that never goes away!

The options are endless. Apart from this book's many other activities that show basic planting, forcing, and other plant concepts, the following are just a very few of the many possibilities.

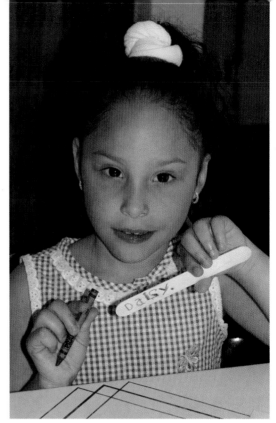

Writing out plant names is educational as well as useful.

Seed Exploration

Seeds are fascinating. They all look different, they do not look anything like what they grow into, and yet they grow into the right plant every time. You can discuss how people grow and talk about each child's unique abilities and traits. You can sing the song "Plant a Radish" from the play *The Fantasticks.* There are all kinds of games to play with seeds, and all kinds of crafts. Use your imagination!

Collect seeds from different plants, and then mix them up. Try to guess which seeds are what and what they will grow into. Mark your guesses on the pots, and then plant them. See who is right.

Collect seeds from regular kitchen vegetables. Compare them to the same type of seeds purchased in seed packets. Try sprouting them both to see what will happen.

Seed Dispersal

Seeds are amazing! Each has discovered its own unique way to get from the parent plant out to a patch of soil to call its own.

Some seeds catch the air and fly, such as those of dandelions and money plant.

Some have burrs that grab hold of passing animals.

Some are surrounded by edible pulp, so animals will collect and move them.

Some pop open, such as impatiens seeds, "exploding" seeds away from the parent plant.

There are some good seed dispersal lesson plans online, or just spend some time in nature, watching how seeds get around!

Propagation

Plant grass, radish, or green bean seeds into clear plastic cups with black construction paper wrapped around them. The paper can be removed periodically to observe root growth, both on its own and as it relates to stem and leaf growth.

Planting seeds is the perfect time to describe the plants that will appear and to spell out plant names with younger children. Many common plant names are descriptive, so talking about the name, how to spell it, and what the new plant will look like is natural and educational. Children love to write plant labels, which can be done on wooden craft sticks. This gives children a sense of owner- ship of the plants while rein- forcing spelling and lan- guage skills.

Cut pieces of coleus or pussy willow and put them in water. Watch what hap- pens—how and where they grow roots. Then after a few weeks, root them into soil, so kids can take home plants.

Break off leaves from a jade plant. Let them dry for two or three days, then set the leaves stem side down into slight- ly moist soil. Watch them root.

Dig a crocus bulb out of the soil (careful- ly!) after it has finished flowering. Look to see how it is adding little cormlets on the sides. Talk about how bulbs reproduce.

When the center plant of hen and chicks and bromeliads have grown large, and small- er plants have formed around the exterior, gently cut the chicks or pups away from the plant and plant them somewhere else, either into pots to give away, or in the ground, per- haps to take over the world!

These are just a few of the ways plants can be propagated. Ask kids to see if they can find more.

Germination

Collect seeds from the wild. Open them up and look at them under a microscope, if you can. Try sprouting them. Do some research on what they need to germinate and grow. Amazingly, some seeds need to be chilled or even frozen, some need to be scratched, and some will lie outside for years until they are in a fire, at which point the outer cover will be burned off, allowing them to germinate.

Talk about germination with kids. It's an amazing process. Discuss why some plants are easy to grow and some are more difficult. Try to figure out to what in the environment this char- acteristic has responded.

Phototropism

Using string and a ruler to measure how sun- flowers turn to the sun and how much they can grow in a day is a great way to dis- cuss phototropism, plant growth, human growth, the turning of the planet . . . the possibili- ties are endless.

These daylilies make a great transition between the beach and a home or walkway.

Seashore Gardens

If you have the chance to plant at the shore, lucky you! Do not be discouraged by those who say it's difficult. A "summer house" garden or a few containers to liven up a sandy area are a joy. Even more, kids are in "fun mode" at the beach, and they're looking for diversions. A seashore garden can be just the thing. Make your seashore gardening a family project.

Basic Requirements

First, it's important to know that just because these plants will tolerate seashore conditions does not mean they can be ignored. The annuals will still need to be watered regularly, and the perennials and woody plants will need to be watered well when they first go in, and then mulched and watered in extreme droughts. Just because plants are tough does not mean that you do not need to take care of them.

When planting trees, shrubs, and perennials at the shore, site the plants carefully, matching the plants to their preferred conditions. Ask your kids to help you find out what the plants like. Give them a sense of ownership. Some plants will be happy right out on the dunes (for example, some grasses and stonecrop), while some will need protection from the wind or water-retentive soil (such as statice). Give them as many of their preferences as possible when planting.

Add lots of organic material when planting, unless you know for a fact the plant prefers poor soil. Kids love to add compost or better yet, composted manure. Ways to use poop is one of most kids' favorite discussions! Be honest with yourself about how much care you and your kids are willing to give. Water-needy plants are not good choices if you are only at the beach on the weekends.

If you plant containers, add moisture crystals to a good, rich potting soil every year. Dump out the old potting mix and start fresh each spring. Try to give containers protection from the wind, because

Good Plant Choices

ANNUALS

Black-eyed Susan vine	Petunia
Cockscomb	Rose moss
Gazania	Statice
Geranium	Strawflower
Globe amaranth	Tuberous begonias
Hollyhock	Verbena
Marigold	Zinnia
Passionflower	

PERENNIALS

Bee balm	Lavender
Black-eyed Susan	Lilyturf
Daylily	Mint
Grasses	Ornamental grasses
Hen and chicks	Stonecrop
Hosta	Swamp rose mallow
Lamb's ear	

TREES AND SHRUBS

Apple	Lilac
Blue Atlas cedar	Pussy willow
Blueberry	Weeping mulberry
Butterfly bush	

strong winds can dry out the soil in just a few hours. Let the kids be in charge of checking pots daily for water. A kid-sized watering can is a great way to give kids ownership of their garden, and save you from doing the majority of the work!

Simple Seashore Garden Ideas

A seashore garden is a great thing. Waves of grasses blowing in the breeze, dancing black-eyed Susans, buckets of annuals, and lilacs breaking the sea smell—all scream summer.

If you have a patio, plant up big buckets of flowers to rim the area, and make a flowery break between sun and sea.

Butterfly bush and bee balm planted around a beach house mean the butterflies will join you on your summer vacation.

Kids love small spaces—and weeping shade trees make excellent hiding places.

Shady Hideaway Gardens

Every child longs for a hidden nook of his or her own. (Most adults do, too.) It's easy to take a difficult shady corner and turn it into a garden hideaway, perfect for reading, coloring, or important lollygagging. Nothing is more conducive to the imagination!

Basic Requirements

- A hidden nook or out of the way shady spot
- Good soil or containers in which to plant
- Accessible water
- A child-friendly pathway

Good Plant Choices

FOR FLOOR

Clover

Thyme

FOR "WALLS"

Bamboo

Black-eyed Susan vine

Green bean

Weeping mulberry

FOR ATMOSPHERE

Coleus	Lilyturf
Crocus	Ornamental grasses
Ferns	Snowdrops
Grape hyacinth	Thyme
Hosta	

Other Good Accents

- A bench or hammock
- A small fountain or wall pond
- A small garden shed or toolbox
- A whimsical piece of statuary or anything you love

Simple Hideaway Garden Ideas

Pick a fenced corner of the yard or small garden nook. Remember that adults always want to make these areas bigger, and kids always want to make them smaller. Cave-like is good.

Plant some hedging shrubs to mask or "wall" it, leaving just enough room for an opening. If you use bamboo, you will have to barricade the roots so they do not spread. Steel barriers are best. No, I'm not kidding. It makes a great hideaway, but you *must* contain it. A weeping mulberry in a corner can also work.

Pave the floor with stepping stones interplanted with thyme, for its wonderful smell when stepped on. You could also use clover, mulch, or shade-tolerant grass.

Create a space for your kids to store keepsakes or play supplies, such as a small garden shed, plastic tub, or storage chest. It must be watertight and heavy enough that it will not blow away in a storm or break from heavy snow.

A place to sit, dream, and commune with nature, such as a bench or hammock, is key. Pillows that can be stored in the supply chest are even better. You want your hideaway to be comfortable and inviting.

The sound of running water is an extra special bonus, but it should not be dangerous in any way. A small wall or tabletop fountain with carefully hidden electric is a wonderful addition. But if you have to pick between safety and ambiance, safety always wins!

These are just ideas to get *your* ideas flowing. Work with your children to create their ideal dream hideaway. For some, it is as simple as a large wooden crate tucked into the garden. For others, it is a family construction project. Listen to your kids—talk with them. And have fun!

Planting marigolds in with herbs and vegetables will help to repel insects and will add color to a kitchen garden.

Vegetable Gardens

Vegetable gardens do not have to be large plots of land. You can grow veggies in a hanging basket, a whiskey barrel, or an old tire. You can grow a few tomatoes along a sunny wall or weave green beans into a chain-link fence. As long as you have a sunny corner or container somewhere, you can grow vegetables.

Basic Requirements

Any container that will fit in the spot you have available and has good drainage is appropriate. Any spot in the garden with full sun, very rich organic soil (lots of humus and compost), good drainage, and plenty of water is ideal.

Good Plant Choices

Basil	Mint
Carrot	Parsley
Corn	Pumpkin
Cucumber	Radish
Dill	Squash
Green bean	Thyme
Lettuce	Tomato
Marigold	

Simple Vegetable Garden Ideas

Plant marigolds around vegetables (such as tomatoes and lettuce) that are often bothered by pests as a natural insect and animal repellent.

Basil, cherry tomatoes (which hang), and marigolds in hanging baskets are a favorite of mine.

Corn, beans, and squash make up the traditional Native American Three Sisters planting. The three plants grow together for the benefit of all: The beans add nitrogen to the soil, the corn acts as a support for the beans, and the squash vine shades the soil around the corn, keeping vital moisture in the ground.

Plant tomatoes into old tires that are painted red. (Use non-toxic paint.) For some reason tomatoes grow better near the color red!

Plant a whiskey barrel full of herbs, and keep it near the kitchen door. Be sure to get a barrel with good drainage holes (or drill some), then put some rocks or gravel in the bottom and fill it with composted manure or compost to give your plants as many organic nutrients in the soil as you can.

If you are making a garden plot, pick a level, open, sunny place in the yard. Remove any grass or weeds and turn in lots of compost and composted manure. Plant the tallest things to the north (so all of the plants get light), and water in well. Be sure to keep plants well watered.

Consider making a raised planter bed, which is easier to weed and work in. Large growers such as watermelons, squash, and pumpkins do well in contained, raised beds.

A strawberry pot can hold strawberries or herbs. They're fun to plant and easy to harvest.

Plant a garden filled with the fruits and veggies your family enjoys—especially the kids. Everyone has favorite summer foods. Try to incorporate everyone's favorites so that the whole family will enjoy the fruits of their labor all summer long.

Water gardens, whether inground as this one is or in containers, provide months of enjoyment for kids and adults alike. No one outgrows scanning the water for glimpses of frogs and fish.

Water Gardens

When I was a kid, we kept large buckets full of frog eggs and pondweeds on the back deck. We would change the water every few days from the pond behind our house and watch the tadpoles grow. When they had transformed into frogs, they would jump out of the bucket and make their way back to the pond. Their growth and journey are my earliest memories of the process of life and have had a lasting impact on me. Though, sadly, most of us don't have ponds behind our houses anymore, we can still experience the pleasure of a water garden and learn the lessons to be found there.

Basic Requirements

- A watertight container, large enough to hold at least one plant
- Distilled water, water from a natural source, or tap water that has stood overnight to allow the chlorine to evaporate
- An upturned pot to raise plant pots to the proper height
- Rocks to hold the pot stable in the larger container
- A pump, fountain, or waterfall for movement

Good Plant Choices

Lotus
Water hyacinth
Water lily

Simple Water Garden Ideas

Water gardens can be as big as a built-in pond (there are some wonderful books out there on how to create these), or as small as a whiskey barrel with a liner or even just a big pot.

Water hyacinths need no care. They float on the top of the water and can make a fun water garden all on their own, especially if you add a few goldfish. Plus, goldfish eat mosquito larvae!

Lotuses require a little more care, and you will want to bring them inside for the winter. If you have chosen a hardy variety, make sure that your pond or pool is deep enough for them to survive winter temperatures in your area. The beauty of their flowers and foliage more than make up for the extra care they demand. They need a deep container, with a foot or two of water.

The Chinese created beautiful containers called fish pots—intricately painted shallow pots with fish painted on the interiors—specifically for bringing their water lilies, lotuses, and fish indoors in the winter. Why not bring a pot of water lilies and goldfish into your house this winter?

You will want your water garden to have moving water—still water invites mosquito larvae and algae. Even small containers benefit from a little fountain, waterfall, or pump to keep the water trickling, bubbling, or churning. This is fun to watch, and the sounds of the water splashing or bubbling can be very soothing and a source of great amusement for children of all ages. *Be careful!* Electricity, water, and children should never be together unsupervised!

What fun running under this blue Atlas cedar, which has been trained to create a unique arch over a pathway.

Whimsy Gardens

What is a whimsy garden? Think Dr. Seuss. Think *Where the Wild Things Are.* Think of the patch of crazy flowers and weird-shaped shrubs you visited as often as you could when you were a kid. That's a whimsy garden. It can be as simple as a big patch of dandelions, whose frowsy heads blow in the wind, or as complex as topiary creatures.

Basic Requirements

- A big enough space to start with some strange-looking trees and shrubs
- Knobby, ruffled, blowsy, or variegated plants that make you laugh and are suitable for your space and environment
- A child's imagination and wonder!

Good Plant Choices

ANNUALS

Black-eyed Susan vine	Passionflower
Brazilian verbena	Pink polka dot plant
Cockscomb	Spider flower
Dandelion	Sweet pea
Gazania	Tuberous begonia
Hollyhock	Zinnias
Nasturtium	

PERENNIALS

Black-eyed Susan	Hosta
Ferns	Lamb's ear
Hen and chicks	Swamp rose mallow

TREES AND SHRUBS

Bamboo	Kousa dogwood
Blue Atlas cedar, especially weeping varieties	Magnolia
	Norway spruce
Camellia	Pussy willow
Crape myrtle	Weeping cherry
Harry Lauder's walking stick	Weeping mulberry

Other Accents

- Bed frames
- Bathtubs
- Broken pottery
- Garden gnomes
- Wind chimes
- Driftwood
- Old bowling balls
- Pink flamingos
- Anything you love that makes you laugh (and is weather resistant)

Simple Whimsy Garden Ideas

It's really unfair of me to tell you what good whimsical plants and gardens are. A whimsy garden is a garden that tickles the giggly place inside of you. For one person, it might be bowling balls. For

While also functional, this birdhouse adds a touch of whimsy by sitting at a jaunty angle.

another it might be whirligigs. I know a woman who awoke to fifty pink flamingoes on her front lawn for her fiftieth birthday. She and her seven-year-old neighbor were delighted. The rest of the neighbors were less so. She thinks they look lovely flocked under her weeping cherry tree. I agree.

Topiary adds a sense of whimsy. So do unusually shaped trees. Multicolored flowers are whimsical, especially when planted with something solid that will act as a foil.

Scarecrows or mannequins, old shoes and hats, silly strings of lights, an old chandelier hanging from a tree . . . whatever makes you happy in your garden could be a good idea.

Painted garden walls, irregularly stacked rocks, or arrangements of found items can all add a sense of surprise and wonder to the garden. Surprise and wonder. Delight. Aren't those the things we go to the garden looking for? My wish is that each and every one of you finds this for yourself.

Afterword

There are surely a few wonderful, whimsical gardens or children's museums with environmental components near you. Seek them out and explore them with your children. They will be memories that last a lifetime.

I hope this book has been helpful. I encourage you to make notes, try new things, and discover favorites of your own. Relish the time you spend in the garden with your children and visit other gardens to get new ideas. Flowers and plants are all around us, and when you look at the world through the eyes of a young gardener, the possibilities for inspiration are endless!

If you have questions or comments, please feel free to email me at ckkrezel@yahoo.com. Happy gardening!

In researching this book, besides relying on the help of my amazing, knowledgeable horticultural friends, I discovered the following organizations and Web sites:

Poison Hotlines and
Poisonous Plant Information

The National Capital Poison Center
1-800-222-1222 (24 hour hotline)
www.poison.org/prevent/plants.asp

MedicineNet.com
This site contains a listing of certified poison control centers for each state.
www.medicinenet.com/poison_control_centers/article.htm

U.S. Army Center for Health Promotion and Preventative Medicine's Guide to Toxic Plants
http://chppm-www.apgea.army.mil/ento/PLANT.HTM

**University of Maryland's
HGIC Plant Diagnostics**
http://plantdiagnostics.umd.edu/

Oklahoma State's Digital Diagnostics
www.ento.okstate.edu/ddd/ddd.html

USDA Cooperative State Research, Education, and Extension Service
www.csrees.usda.gov/

Gardening with Children and Children's Gardens in the U.S.

The National Gardening Association
http://www.kidsgardening.com

National Database of Children's Gardens
The American Horticultural Society maintains this database of children's gardens at public gardens to encourage interaction and enjoyment of these educational spaces.
www.ahs.org/horticulture_internet_community/national_registry_of_childrens_gardens.htm

Lady Bird Johnson Wildflower Center
www.wildflower2.org

Common Name Index

Botanical Name Index